TUDOR TOWNSCAPES

Tudor Townscapes

THE TOWN PLANS FROM JOHN SPEED'S

Theatre of the Empire of Great Britaine 1610

Introduced and with Commentaries by

JEFFERY JOHN SPEED

MAP COLLECTOR PUBLICATIONS · 2000

Published by Map Collector Publications Ltd, Waddesdon, Bucks, England HP18 0JL
with generous support from Kerr-McGee North Sea (UK) Ltd
© Jeffery John Speed 2000
All rights reserved
ISBN 0 906430 22 4 (hardback) 250 copies
ISBN 0 906430 23 2 (paperback) 750 copies

Cover/Jacket: Speed's plan of London
Title-page: Portrait of John Speed engraved by S. Savery, 1631

Typeset in C & C 'Galliard'
Printed in Great Britain by Balding+Mansell Ltd
Norwich NR6 5DR

CONTENTS

CONTENTS

FOREWORD

My interest in John Speed started in my early teens when I consulted the school copy of Encyclopaedia Britannica to find out if our family might have any illustrious connections with the past. The thought of possible descent from the creator of the great early English maps was exciting and intriguing.

I knew that my paternal great grandfather had been born in Jamaica in 1848 where his father had been an Attorney-at-Law in Portland parish, and that my great-uncle had traced these Jamaican family records back to the early 1700s.

John Speed the cartographer was born in 1552 at Farndon in Cheshire, on the borders of Wales, and during his 77 years fathered 18 children (12 of them sons) by one devoted wife – Susanna. According to Cheshire records, Samuel Speed (one of his grandsons) became implicated in a plot against Cromwell and was forced to leave the country. He went to the West Indies where he joined some buccaneers and later became 'a famous and valiant sea-chaplain and seaman'.

There would seem to be a strong probability that this Samuel Speed was the great-grandfather of my ancestor Joseph Speed who was born in Jamaica in 1728. Thus I believe that I am one of John Speed's direct descendants through twelve generations. However I have not inherited his fecundity !   J.J.S

ACKNOWLEDGMENTS

My first thanks must be to those who encouraged my early interest in John Speed and his maps. Principal among these was the late James Forrest (Donald) Baird, and the doyen of the cartographic world, the late Ronald Vere Tooley.

This publication would have been impossible without the generous support and friendship of Frank Sharratt of Kerr-McGee Oil, and the expertise of Iain Bain.

The magnificent copy of John Speed's *Theatre* from which all the coloured illustrations are taken, is in the library of Trinity College, Cambridge. I am much indebted to the Master and Fellows for their permission to make use of it, and to the librarian Dr David McKitterick for his help and for his note on the book's provenance.

The transcription of John Speed's original text and general editorial advice was undertaken by my wife Hilary, to whom I owe so much, but any errors or omissions are mine (or my ancestor's).

INTRODUCTION

When maps and mapmakers are being discussed, particularly the early English cartographers, the name that is best known and one of the most respected is that of the Cheshire merchant tailor and historian, John Speed.

His writings encompassed religion, history and geography, but it is for his *Theatre of theEmpire of Great Britaine* that he is most celebrated. This work was a huge success, with its uniquely decorative maps of all the English and Welsh counties and the Irish provinces, as well as a general map of Scotland.

The 'Theatre' (a term first used by the Flemish cartographer Abraham Ortelius for his great world atlas in 1570) was published fully in 1611 or 1612, and ran to at least four editions during Speed's lifetime. After his death in 1629 the atlas continued to be in demand, and there were four further issues of the work up to 1676, when the last main edition of the *Theatre* was published.

The eight editions referred to above included a description and historical notes for each county, but the maps were also printed and sold as single sheets, without the descriptive text on the reverse. Participants in the Civil War in the mid-17th century found these invaluable.

Bound collections of the maps, also without text, were issued at various times and the last of these (published by C.Dicey & Co.) appeared as late as 1770, a remarkable 160 years after the first edition. The copperplates were amended, retouched and repaired during this long period, but the maps seem to have been commercially viable to the end.

The atlases, and the individual maps, have been prized by collectors, scholars and historians for nearly four hundred years, and as we enter their fifth century, demand remains as strong as ever and prices continue to lead the market. John Speed's maps were the first to contain within them plans and bird's-eye views of the main county towns and cities. Most of these town-plans were drawn by Speed and based on his own surveys. They provide delightful illustrations of urban life in Tudor times.

The maps have been reproduced often, but the town plans have not been reprinted separately, nor enlarged to enable their full detail and charm to be appreciated. It is the aim of this book to mark the Millennium by providing readily accessible copies of all these plans, at a scale which will show more clearly the accuracy and value of John Speed's surveys, and enable our heritage to be more fully understood.

EDITORIAL NOTE

The dramatic colours in the illustrations are true to the magnificent original Atlas from Trinity College, Cambridge, and provide a unique view of what could be achieved by the very best colourists at the time of the book's publication. The history of this remarkable copy follows this note. Very occasional stains or blemishes in the originals have been left as they are, without retouching; a small amount missing from a corner of the plan of Newport has been made good from another source in black-and-white .

Each of the 72 Town Plans that appear on the county maps in John Speed's atlas have been enlarged to as great an extent as possible on the page size of this book, whilst retaining the original proportions. This means that the plans that are relatively smaller in the original, have been more greatly magnified.

The descriptive text which appeared on the reverse of the maps, has been taken unaltered (except as noted below) from the 1676 edition of the atlas, but the order of paragraphs has in many cases been changed to give prominence to the copy that relates to the particular town. Where the description of the town is brief some detail of the surrounding county is also included.

The original text is littered with errors and variations in spelling, as well as sentences that are difficult to comprehend. I have chosen the text of the last and largest edition of the atlas because there had been some correction and improvement compared to the earlier editions. The eight main editions from 1611 to 1676 were published with text and this was re-set for each edition. There were at least four further issues of the atlas but those maps all had plain backs.

The principal change I have made to the text is to substitute the round letter *s* in place of the long ſ used by printers until the end of the 18th century. I have also, as sparingly as possible, put clarifications or corrections in square brackets – thus [ ]. Several words which occur regularly and whose meaning is clear from their context I have left untouched. Examples are 'Country' (where County is intended), 'thorow' for through, and 'daies' for days. Capital letters were used in a rather haphazard fashion, and punctuation likewise.

John Speed's style certainly has great charm and some of his anecdotes are delightful. His preoccupation with references to earlier historians is unsurprising, bearing in mind that he was concurrently writing his magnum opus – *The History of Great Britaine*. He was an honourable exception, in an age when plagiarism was rife, in frequently citing his sources and giving them due regard. This was particularly evident on his county maps, and the town plans that were based on his own surveys are those which bear a 'Scale of Paces'.

In his foreword to the Atlas he readily acknowledges his debt to earlier scholars, and his disarming modesty makes much stronger the certainty that about 50 of the plans were indeed his own work. This foreword is here reprinted in full to provide a graphic and revealing insight into the character of this great and good Englishman.

THE PROVENANCE OF THE ATLAS USED FOR ILLUSTRATING THIS BOOK

The illustrations in this book are taken from a specially coloured copy of Speed's *Theatre*. It belonged originally to Anne of Denmark, wife of King James I, and was quite possibly a present to her by Speed himself. Queen Anne died in 1619, but the book may have left her library before then. Her son Prince Henry, elder brother of the future Charles I, died, widely mourned, in November 1612. With him died the hopes not just of his courtiers, but also of a carefully nurtured learned culture. His tutor was Adam Newton, a Scotsman admired for his skill in the classical languages, whose subsequent career was perforce to be outside the royal households. Newton's home was Charlton House, on the escarpment overlooking the Thames just downstream from Greenwich. Built by Newton in 1607-12, and one of the finest surviving Jacobean buildings in London, it still retains something of the open outlook that was much valued in the seventeenth century. Among Newton's books were several that had once belonged to Prince Henry, and this exceptional volume from the library of his mother. These books passed by descent to Sir Henry Puckering, who presented virtually his entire library to Trinity College between the early 1690s and his death in 1701. The copy of Speed has been in the College library ever since.

The Queen's love of fine things was well known. Daughter of Frederick II, King of Norway and Denmark, and elder sister of Christian IV of Denmark, she married James VI of Scotland (as he then was) in 1589. In England, her tastes developed, not only for jewellery, fine clothes and dancing, but also for masques. She took part in some of those devised by Ben Jonson and Inigo Jones, and encouraged many more. In 1611 she was granted the palace of Oatlands, about twenty miles upstream on the Thames from London, and in 1614 she was granted that of Greenwich as well, though she did not live to see its rebuilding completed. Her architectural interests were given rein as she worked with Inigo Jones at Greenwich, and she was also partly responsible for alterations at Somerset House. She died heavily in debt.

Her copy of Speed, in which the *Theatre* and the *History* are bound up together, as was intended, is bound in red leather, densely covered with gilt decorations. The binding has been attributed to the so-called 'Squirrel Binder', after a distinctive tool that he used. Other books by the same binding shop are to be found among the libraries of James I, Prince Henry and Charles I and it seems that his career spanned from the beginning of the century until the late 1630s. In the centre of the cover is the Queen's armorial shield. Because the book is so fat (it is now about 14cm. thick), the pages and maps were each thrown out on guards, in order that the pages could be read and enjoyed without the reader's having to peer into the gutter. This makes it still more bulky.

Inside the book is gorgeously decorated. The wealth of ornament and illustration in Speed's books already made them expensive, but this copy has been embellished still more elaborately. The engraved title-page sets the tone, coloured and heightened with gold to an exceptional standard. It is immediately followed by the elaborate engraving by Jodocus Hondius of the arms of James I (to whom the *Theatre* was dedicated) surrounded by the shields of earlier monarchs. Decorations, pictures of coins and other small illustrations are coloured as well, often also with gold. So too are the maps of which details are reproduced in the present volume.

The map of Cambridgeshire clearly shows the magnificence that was achieved in the finest of Speed's maps. The scale of this illustration is about one-sixteenth of the original. The enlarged town plan of the city of Cambridge is shown on p.33.

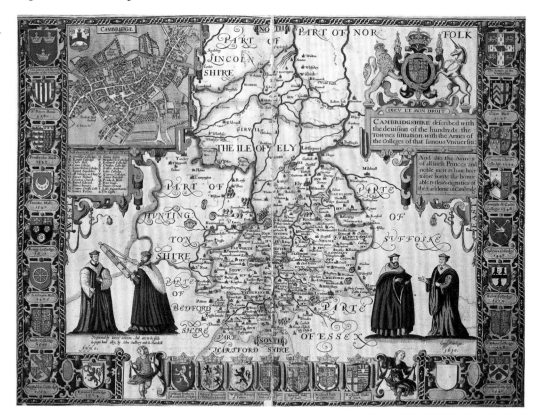

THE EDITIONS OF JOHN SPEED'S ATLAS

The Town Plans reproduced in this book have all been taken from the 1616 (Latin text) edition of the Atlas kindly made available by Trinity College, Cambridge. Details of its historic provenance have already been noted. The contemporary hand colouring is a dramatic feature of this royal Atlas, and splendidly illustrates the abilities of the very best colourists of the early 17th century. The main editions of the Atlas are listed below.

1610 The First Edition, published by John Sudbury and George Humble. The actual date of this publication is open to doubt as many of the plates bear the date 1610, but the title page of the Atlas shows 1611 and the intermediate title pages for the Third Book (Scotland) and the Fourth Book (Ireland) give 1612.

1614 The Second Edition was almost identical to the First, but the English text on the reverse of the maps had been completely reset, and the edition was almost certainly issued in 1616, which date appears on two of the intermediate title pages, although the main title gives 1614.

1616 The Third Edition, and the only one to have Latin text throughout, although the maps are identical to the Second Edition

1627 The Fourth Edition, published by George Humble alone. There is evidence of a (projected?) edition of 1623 which had the same text as the 1614 edition, but additions and corrections to the engraved plates. The 1627 edition was issued with the First Edition of Speed's *Prospect of the most famous parts of the World*, and was the last publication before his death in 1629 at the age of 77.

1632   The Fifth Edition, almost indistinguishable from the Fourth, but issued with the Second Edition of the *Prospect*, and with re-set text.

1646   The Sixth Edition, now published by William Humble, son of George. The text has again been re-set, and this is often the only indication of the edition to which a particular map belongs. William Humble seems to have had several different chronological dates on title pages of his publishing, but these did not constitute definitive editions.

1662   The Seventh Edition, published by Roger Rea the Elder and Younger. Although the title page of the *Theatre* is dated 1650, it was issued together with the *Prospect* which was dated 1662. All of the county maps had their imprints changed on the plates for this edition.

1676   The Eighth Edition, published by Thomas Bassett and Richard Chiswell whose imprint replaced the previous one on every map. This was the last edition of the Atlas with text, issued after the Great Fire of London.

Further editions or published collections of Speed's county maps were produced in 1695 by Christopher Browne, in 1713 and 1743 by Henry Overton, and in 1770 by Cluer Dicey & Co..

JOHN SPEED'S ORIGINAL INTRODUCTION

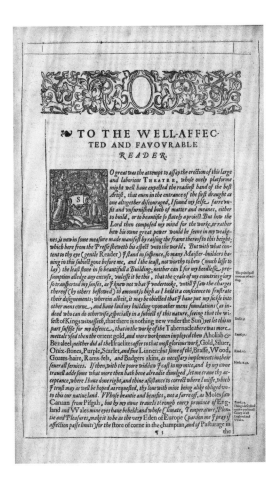

'To the Well-Affected and favourable Reader.

So great was the attempt to assay the erection of this large and laborious THEATRE, whose only platform might well have expected the readiest hand of the best Artist, that even in the entrance of the first draught, as one altogether discouraged, I found myself far unfit, and unfurnished both of matter and means, either to build, or to beautifie so stately a project. But how the Lord then composed my mind for the work, or rather how his own great power would be seen in my weakness, is now in some measure made manifest by raising the frame thereof to this height, which here from the Press sheweth his aspect unto the World.

But with what content to thy eye (Gentle Reader) I stand in suspence, so many Master-builders having in this Subject gone before me, and I the least, not worthy to hew (much less to lay) the least Stone in so beautiful a Building: neither can I for my heedless presumption alledge any excuse, unless it be this, that the zeal of my Countries glory so transported my senses, as I knew not what I undertook, until I saw the charges thereof (by others bestowed) to amount so high, as I held it a conscience to frustrate their designments; wherein albeit, it may be objected that I have put my Sickle into other mens Corn, and have laid my Building upon other mens Foundations, (as indeed who can do otherwise, especially in a Subject of this nature, seeing that the Wisest of Kings witnesseth, that there is nothing new under the Sun;) yet let this in part suffice for my defence, that in the work of the Tabernacle there were more metals used than the Orient Gold, and more Workmen imployed than Aholiab and Bezaleel; neither did all the Israelites offer to that most glorious Work, Gold, Silver, Onyx-stones, Purple, Scarlet and Fine Linnen: but some of them Brass, Wood, Goats-hair, Rams-fells, and Badgers-skins, as necessary implements in their several services.

If then, with the poor Widow, I cast in my mite, and by my own travel add somewhat more than hath been already divulged, let me crave thy acceptance where I have done right, and thine assistance to correct where I miss; which I trust may as well be hoped as requested, thy love with mine being alike obliged unto this our native Land. Whose beauty and benefits, not afar off, as Moses saw Canaan from Pisgah, but by mine own travels through every Province of England and Wales, mine eyes have beheld: and whose Climate, Temperature, Plenty and Pleasures, make it to be as the very Eden of Europe (pardon me I pray, if affection pass limits) for the store of Corn in the Champian, and of pasturage in the lower Grounds, presseth the Cart under the sheaves to the Barn, and filleth the Coffers of their Possessors.

Neither are the faces of the Mountains and Hills only spread over with infinite Herds and sorts of Cattel, but their intrals also are in continual travel, and continually delivered of their rich Progenies of Copper, Lead, and Iron, Marble, Christal, Jet, Alabaster, yea, the most wonder-working Loadstone; to say nothing either of Cannol and Sea-coal, as rich for profit, and as needful for use; or of the goodly quarries of choicest Stone, as necessary for Strength, as estimable for Beauty. Her Seas and Rivers so stored with Fish, and her Fells and Fens so replenished with wild Fowl, that they even present themselves ready for prey to their takers: briefly, every Soil is so enriched with Plenty and Pleasures, as the Inhabitants think there is no other Paradise, in the Earth but where themselves dwell.

The true plot of the whole Land, and that again into parts in several Cards are here described, as likewise the Cities and Shire-Towns are inserted; whereof some have been performed by others, without Scale annexed, the rest by mine own travels; and unto them for distinction sake, the Scale of Paces, accounted according to the Geometrical measure, five foot to a pace I have set; but in this employment I am somewhat to excuse my self from wrongs conceived done unto more beautiful and richer Corporations, which in this survey are in silence over-passed, and places of less note and frequency described:

For satisfaction whereof, (good Reader) understand my purpose, according to the Title prefixed, which in this Island (besides other things) is to shew the situation of every City and Shire-Town only. So that without injury to all, I could not insert some, though oftentimes it grieved me much to leave such beautiful places untouched: which notwithstanding being well known so to be, giveth no little glory to the Land in general, so to be replenished with store and choice, as hardly can be judged which may be omitted.

The Shires divisions into Lathes, Hundreds, Wapentakes, and Cantreds, according to their ratable and accustomed manner, I have separated, and under the same Title that the record beareth, in their due places distinguished; wherein by the help of the Tables annexed, any City, Town, Burrough, Hamlet, or place of note may readily be found, and whereby safety may be affirmed, that there is not any one Kingdom in the World so exactly described, as is this our island of GREAT-BRITAIN, that only accepted which Josuah conquered, and into Tribes divided.

The Arms of such Princes and Nobles as have had the dignities, and born the Titles either of Dukes, Marquesses, or Earls, in the same Province, City, or Place: and finally, the Battles fought either by the Forrain or home-bred Conspirators, I have also added. Where we from under our own Vines, without fear, may behold the Prints of endured miseries, sealed with the blood of those times, to the loss of their lives and liberties; our selves (as in the reign of Augustus, when the Temple of Janus stood shut, and Mars his hands bound with Chains of Brass, as Virgil speaketh) hear not the sound of the Alarum in our Gates, nor the clattering of Armour in our Camps, whose Swords are now tuned into Mattocks, and Spears into Sithes, as Micah sheweth the peaceable times under Christ.

In shewing these things, I have chiefly sought to give satisfaction to all, without offence to any, whereof if I fail, yet this to my self have I gained, that whilst I set all my thoughts and cogitations hereon, I had small regard to the bewitching pleasures and vain enticements of this wicked world, neither had I leisure to be led by an ambitious desire to raise my station above the level of my equals, or with base flattery to follow, and fill the ears of Fortunes Deputies, the reins of these intents, checking the bit of affection into another way. And applying my self wholly to the frame of this most goodly Building, have as a poor Labourer carried the carved Stones, and polished Pillars, from the hands of the more skilful Architects, to be set in their fit places, which here I offer upon the Altar of Love to my Country, and wherein I have held it no Sacriledge to rob others of their richest Jewels to adorn this my most beautiful Nurse, whose Womb was my Conception, whose Breasts were my Nourishment, whose Bosom my Cradle, and Lap (I doubt not) shall be my bed of sweet Rest, till Christ by his Trumpet raise me thence.

1 Chron. 28.8 Therefore in the sight of the Congregation of the Lord, and the audience of our God, let us keep and seek for all the Commandments of the Lord our God, that we may possess this good Land, and leave it for an inheritance for our Children after us for ever.

Thine in Christ Jesus,
JOHN SPEED.

T H E

Theatre of the Empire
OF

GREAT-BRITAIN,

Presenting an Exact Geography of the
KINGDOM of ENGLAND, SCOTLAND, IRELAND,
and the ISLES adjoyning:

As also the Shires, Hundreds, Cities and Shire-Towns within the KINGDOM
of ENGLAND and PRINCIPALITY of WALES;

WITH A

Chronology of the Civil-wars in ENGLAND, WALES and IRELAND.

TOGETHER WITH

A PROSPECT

Of the most Famous Parts of the WORLD, Viz.

Asia, Africa, Europe, America.

With these EMPIRES and KINGDOMS therein contained; viz.

Grecia,	France,	Hungary,	Turkish-Empire,
Roman-Empire,	Belgia,	Denmark,	Kingdom of China.
Germany,	Spain,	Poland,	Tartaria,
Bohemia.	Italy,	Persia,	Summer-Islands.

By JOHN SPEED.

In this New Edition are added;
In the THEATRE of GREAT-BRITAIN,

The Principal Roads, and their Branches leading to the Cities and chief Towns in *England* and *Wales*; with their computed distances. In a new and accurate method.

The Market Towns wanting in the former Impressions.
A Continuation of all the Battels fought in *England, Scotland, Wales* and *Ireland*; with all the Sea-Fights to this present time.

The Arms of all the Dukes and Earls, whose Titles of Honour were wanting in each particular County, to the last Creation.

The Descriptions of His Majesty's Dominions abroad; with a Map fairly engraven to each Description,

Viz. { New-England, | Carolina, | Virginia, | Jamaica,
      { New-York, | Florida, | Mary-Land, | Barbadoes.

In the PROSPECT of the WORLD.
The Empire of the Great Mogul, } Palestine, or the Holy-Land,
with the rest of the East-Indies. } The Empire of Russia.

LONDON;

Printed for *Thomas Basset* at the *George* in *Fleet-street*, and *Richard Chiswel*
at the *Rose* and *Crown* in St. *Paul's* Church-yard, MDCLXXVI.

BATH

'This Country [Somerset] is famoused by 3 Cities, Bathe, Wells, and Bristow. The first takes name of the hot Baths, which Antonine called Aquae Solis, the Water of the Sun; Stephen, Badiza; we at this day Bathe, and the Latinists Bathonia; a place of continual concourse for persons of all degrees, and almost of all diseases, (whence it was sometimes called Akeman-cester) who by divine providence do very often find relief there, the Springs thereof by reason of their Mineral and sulphurous passage, being of such exceeding power and medicinal heat, as they cure and conquer the rebellious stubbornness of corrupt humors, in respect of which admirable virtues some have fabled, that they were first conveyed by Magick Art. To testifie the antiquity of this place, many Images and Roman Inscriptions are found in the Walls, which can now be hardly read, they are so worn and eaten into by age.

The air is mild and pleasing, and for the most part subject to such temperate dispositions as the Summer-season affordeth, whence some have erroniously conceited that the Region borrowed her name from the nature of her Clime: yet how delightful soever it is in the time of Summer, with change of the season it may well change her pleasing name, and borrow some winterly denomination; so full of wet, so myry and moorish it is; insomuch as the Inhabitants can hardly travel to and fro without their great incumbrance.

Howbeit they pass over this with all patience, knowing their ensuing seasonable profits far to exceed any present detriments and displeasures: for as it is foul, so it is fruitful, which makes them comfort themselves with this Proverb, that What is worst for the Rider is best for the Abider: the Soil and Glebe thereof being very fertile, and every side garnished with Pastures and delightful Meadows and beautified with Mannor-houses both many and fair; and (in a word) hath everything in it to content the purse, the heart, the eye at home: and sufficient Ports to give entertainment to Commodities from abroad.

The ancient Inhabitants that possess this Province were the Belgae, who spread themselves far and wide, as well here as in Wilt-shire and the inner parts of Hamp-shire; who being branched from the Germans, conferred the names of those places from whence they came, upon these their seats where they resided.'

¶ As published, within Speed's map of Somerset, this is the largest of the plans, and therefore the least enlarged in this volume. The origin of the survey is uncertain, but possibly it was by Dr John Jones in 1572, when he wrote on thermal waters (the prominence of five baths inset tends to support this provenance). Note also on the plan the Horse Bath just south of the city walls, complete with occupant!

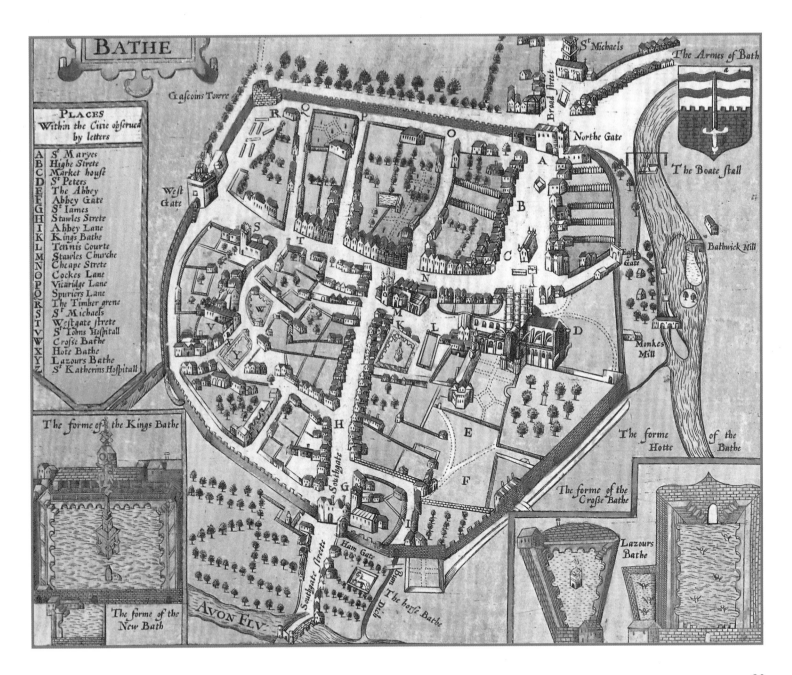

BATHE

The Armes of Bath

The Boate stall

Gascoins Towre

Northe Gate

West Gate

St Michaels

Broad Street

Bathwick Mill

Monkes Mill

The forme of the Hotte Bathe

The forme of the Crosse Bathe

Lazours Bathe

The forme of the Kings Bathe

The forme of the New Bath

AVON FLV.

Southgate Strete

Southgate

Ham Gate

Bum The horse Bathe

PLACES
Within the Citie obserued
by letters

A   St Maryes
B   Highe Strete
C   Market house
D   St Peters
E   The Abbey
F   Abbey Gate
G   St Iames
H   Stawles Strete
I   Abbey Lane
K   Kings Bathe
L   Tennis Courte
M   Stawles Churche
N   Cheape Strete
O   Cockes Lane
P   Vicaridge Lane
Q   Spuriers Lane
R   The Timber grene
S   St Michaels
T   Westgate strete
V   St Iohns Hospitall
W   Crosse Bathe
X   Hote Bathe
Y   Lazours Bathe
Z   St Katherins Hospitall

BEDFORD

'This Town by the Britains was called Lettidur; by the Saxons Bedanpord; and of us Bedford: being the chiefest in the County, from whom it taketh the name, and is most fruitful, and pleasantly seated, having the Ouse running thorow the Town in the midst, and a fair Stone-bridge built over the same, whereon are two Gates to lock and impeach the passage, as occasion shall serve. At the first entrance standeth S.Leonards Hospital for Lazars: and further inwards S.Johns and S.Maries Churches: within the Town S.Pauls, a most beautiful Church, S.Cuthberts, and S.Peters: without the Town standeth the Fryers, S.Loyes, Alhallows, and Caudwell Abby: not far whence, sometimes stood a Chapel upon the Bank of Ouse, wherein (as Florilegus affirmeth) the body of Offa the great Mercian King was interred, but by the overswelling of that River was born down, and swallowed up: whose Tomb of Lead (as it were some phantastical thing) appeared often to them that seek it not, but to them that seek it (sayeth Rosse) it is invisible. This Town is governed yearly by a Mayor, two Bayliffs, two Chamberlains, a Recorder, a Town-clerk, and three Sergeants with Maces.

Castles in this Shire are Woodhill, Eaton, Temsford, and Amphill, an honour now appertaining to the Crown. And places of Religion built by devout persons, but for Idolatrous abuses again abolished, were at Bedford, Harwood, Helenstow, Newenham, Chicksand, Wardon, Woborn and Dunstable. All these, with their like, felt the hand of Henry the eighth to lie so heavy upon them, that they were not able to sustain the weight, but were crushed to pieces, and fell to the ground.

The Graduation of this County, taken for the Shire-Town, is placed from the Equator in the degree of 52, and 30 minutes for latitude, and is removed from the first West point of longitude 20 degrees and 16 minutes.' ❧

¶ The plan is clear and easily recognisable as that part of the present town that straddles the River Ouse. Although it contains no remarkable features or decoration, the arms of the town are neatly and uniquely incorporated into the title.

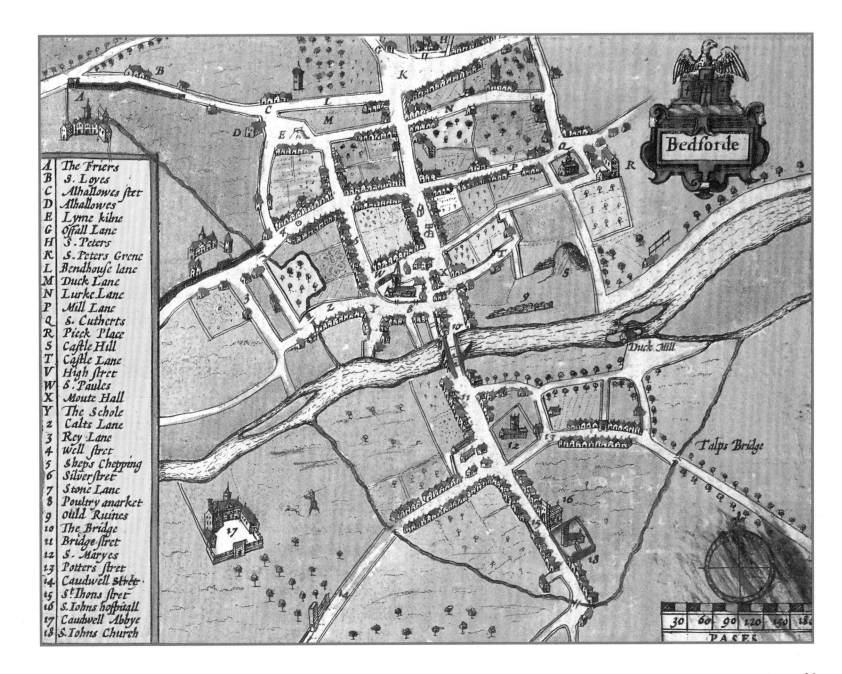

A	The Friers
B	S. Loyes
C	Alhallowes stret
D	Alhallowes
E	Lyme kilne
G	Offall Lane
H	S. Peters
K	S. Peters Grene
L	Bendhouse lane
M	Duck Lane
N	Lurke Lane
P	Mill Lane
Q	S. Cutherts
R	Pieck Place
S	Castle Hill
T	Castle Lane
V	High stret
W	S. Paules
X	Moute Hall
Y	The Schole
Z	Calts Lane
3	Rey Lane
4	Well stret
5	Sheps Chepping
6	Silver stret
7	Stone Lane
8	Poultry market
9	ould Ruines
10	The Bridge
11	Bridge stret
12	S. Maryes
13	Potters stret
14	Caudwell stret
15	S. Ihons stret
16	S. Iohns hospitall
17	Caudwell Abbye
18	S. Iohns Church

Bedforde

Duck Mill

Talps Bridge

30 60 90 220 150 18

PASES

25

BERWICK

'The utmost Town in England, and the strongest hold in all Britain is Barwick From whence it had the name is not certainly made known. Some fetch it from Berengarius a Duke (never read of): some say it was called Beornica-pic in the old English-Saxon tongue, which is the Town of the Bernicians. Howsoever, this is better to be said then trusted: and whencesoever it hath the name, it is seated between two mighty Kingdoms, shooting far into the Sea, with which, and the River Tweed, it is almost encompassed: and whensoever any discord fell between the two Nations, this place was the first thing they took care of. It hath indured the brunts of divers inroads and incursions, and been oftentimes both possessed and repossessed of the Scots and English. But since it was reduced under the command of Edward the fourth, our Kings have from time to time so strengthened it with new works and fortifications, as they cut off all hopes of winning it. The Governor of this Town is also Warden of the East Marches against Scotland. The longitude of it according to Mathematical observations, is 21 degrees and 43 minutes: the latitude 55 degrees and 48 minutes.

The air must needs be subtle and piercing, for that the Northernly parts are most exposed to extremity of weathers, as great winds, hard frosts, and long lying of Snows, &c. Yet would it be far more sharp then it is, were not the German Seas a ready means to further the dissolution of her Ice and Snow, and the plenty of Coals there gotten, a great help to comfort the body with warmth, and defend the bitter coldness.

The soil cannot be rich, having neither fertility of ground for Corn or Cattle, the most part of it being rough, and in every place hard to be manured, save only towards the Sea and River Tyne, where by the great diligence and industrious pains of good husbandry, that part is become very fruitful'. 🐎

¶ This fine plan was based on an earlier drawing in the collection of Sir Robert Cotton, but the inclusion of a scale of paces shows that Speed had carried out his own survey, perhaps to augment the information to hand and certainly ascertain measurements. Note that the orientation is moved 45 degrees to the left, and the essential fortifications of this strategic border town are prominent

	KEY
A	Castle
B	Whyte wall
C	S.Marie gate
D	Bell Tower
E	Lordes mount
F	The Grenes
G	West mount
H	New Marie gate
I	Middle mount
K	Search:house mount
L	Cow: gate
M	Mill mount
N/O	2 Store houses
P	Hunsdons new mount
Q	Hunsdons mount
R	Pallace Tower
S	Copons Tower
T	Shore-gate
V	Maison deeu
W	Bridge gate
Y	Kinges Stables
X	Tolebooth and state-house
Z	Parado
I	Pallace

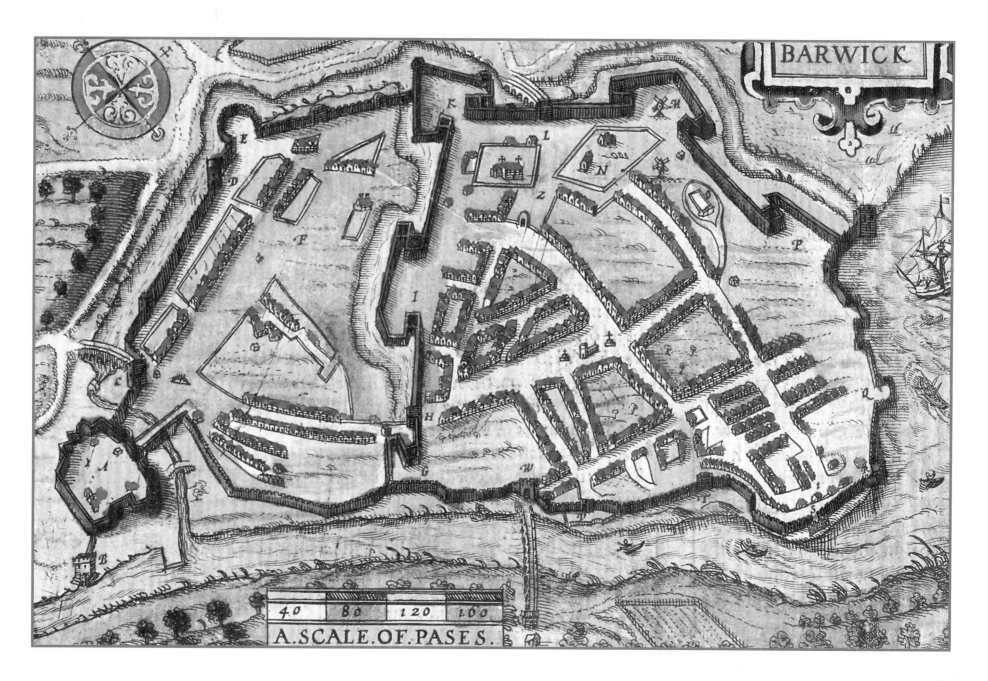

BARWICK

A.SCALE.OF.PASES.

40   80   120   160

27

BRISTOL

'Bristow is one of the greatest and famous Cities in England, the greatest parte therof standeth in ye boundes of Glocestershire ye rest in Somersettshire: but the Bristollians will nott be counted in eyther, but will be a County or Shire within themselfes. It standeth upon the River of Avon, which 4 myles from thenc falleth into Severn, it hath a fayre bridge of stone with howses on each side like London bridge and almost halfe so long although but 4 Arches. In the East end of ye Citty is ye Castle, which they confes to stand in Glocestershire. Ther is no dunghill in all ye Cittie nor any sinke that cometh from any house into ye Streets but all is conveyed underground, neyther have they any Carts, but cary all upon Sledds. There is in ye Citty and Suburbs 20 fayre Churches whereof 18 are parish Churches. It is governed by a Mayor, Aldermen and Shirifs having Swoord and wearing Scarlett as they doe in Glocester, London and other Citties upon great high and feastivall dayes in ye yeare. A towne of great Merchandise. The chiefe Kay standeth upon ye lesser River called Froome which ebbeth and floweth some tymes 40 foote in height bringing in Shipps of very great burden. The Castle was builded by Robert Consul of Glocester, bastard sonne of Kinge Henry the first.

The ground of this Shire throughout yieldeth plenty of corn and bringeth forth abundance of fruits; the one through the natural goodness only of the ground, the other through the diligent manuring and tillage, in such wise, that it would provoke the laziest person to take pains. Here you may see the High-wayes and common Lanes clad with Apple-trees and Pear-trees, not engrafted by the industry of mans hand, but growing naturally of their own accord: the ground of it self is so inclined to bear fruits and those both in tast and beauty far exceeding others, and will endure until a new supply come. There is not any Country [county] in England so thick set with Vineyards as this Province is, so plentiful of increase, and so pleasant in taste. The very Wines made thereof carry no unpleasant tartness, as being little inferior in sweet verdure to the French Wines. The houses are innumerable, the Churches passing fair, and the Towns standing very thick. But that which addeth unto all good gifts (a special glory) is the River Severn, than which there is not any in all the Land for Chanel broader, for Stream swifter, or for fish better stored. There is in it a daily rage and fury of Waters, which I know not whether I may call a Gulf or Whirlpool of Waves, raising up the sands from the bottom, winding and driving them upon heaps: sometimes overflowing her banks, roveth a great way upon the face of her bordering grounds, and again retireth as a Conqueror into the usual Chanel. Unhappy is the Vessel which it taketh full upon the side; but the Water-men wellware thereof, when they see that Hydra coming, turn the Vessel upon it, and cut thorow the midst of it, whereby they check and avoid her violence and danger.'

John Speed was quite properly impressed with Bristol's importance and situation. He used the plan published by Braun and Hogenberg in 1581, and they had used the survey of 1568 by William Smith. Speed's description includes fascinating detail of civilised life in the Tudor city.

KEY

A	Great St Augustin
B	LittleSt Augustin
C	The Gaunte
D	St Michaell
E	St Iames
F	Froomgate
G	St Iohns
H	St Lawrence
I	St Stephens
K	St Leonard
L	St Warburgs
M	Christ chirch
N	Allhallowes
O	St Mary port
P	St Peters
Q	St Phillip
R	The Castle
S	St Nicholas
T	St Thomas
V	The Temple
W	Ratcliffe Gate
X	Temple gate
Y	Newgate

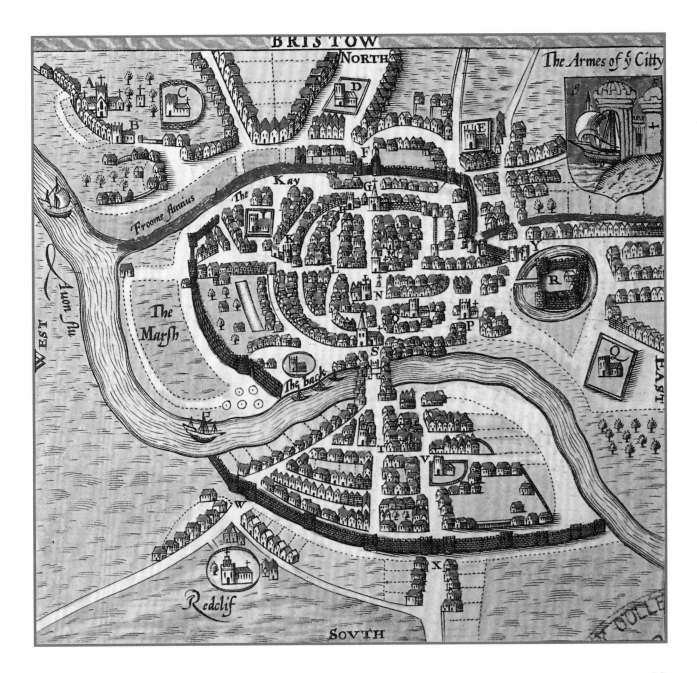

BUCKINGHAM

'The Shire-town Buckingham, fruitfully seated upon the River Ouse, was fortified with a Rampire, and sconces on both banks, by King Edward the elder, sayeth Marianus the Scotish Writer; where in the heart of the Town hath stood a strong Castle, mounted upon an high hill, which long since was brought to the period of her estate, now nothing remaining but the signs that there she had stood.

The River circulates this Town on every side, that only upon the North excepted, over which three fair stone-bridges lead, and into which the springs of a Well run, called Saint Rumalds, a Child-saint born at Kings-Sutton, canonized, and in the Church of this Town enshrined, with many conceited miracles and cures: such was the hap of those times, to produce Saints of all ages and sexes.

This Town is governed by a Bailiff and twelve principal Burgesses; and is in the degree removed from the first point of the West for Longitude 19.33.scruples; and the North-pole elevated in Latitude for the degree 52.18 scruples. The air is passing good, temperate and pleasant, yielding the Body Health and the Mind Content. The Soil is rich, fat, and fruitful, giving abundance of Corn, Grass, and Marle.

Buckinghamshire is chiefly divided into two parts by the Chiltren hills, which run thorow this Shire in the midst, and before time were so pestered with Beech, that they were altogether unpassable, and became a recepticle and refuge for theeves, who daily endammaged the way-faring man; for which cause Leostan Abbot of Saint Albans caused them to be cut down: since when those parts are passable, without any great incumbrances of trees; from whose tops a large and most pleasing prospect is seen.

The Vale beneath is plain and champion, a clayie Soil, stiff, and rough, but withall marvellous fruitful, naked of Woods, but abounding in Meadows, Pastures and Tillage, and maintaining an infinite number of Sheep, whose soft and fine fleeces are in great esteem with the Turks, as far as Asia.'

¶ A charming representation of the small county town, with appropriately rural embellishments. The seasons seem to overlap somewhat, with ploughing and sowing apparently taking place at the same time as reaping and harvesting.

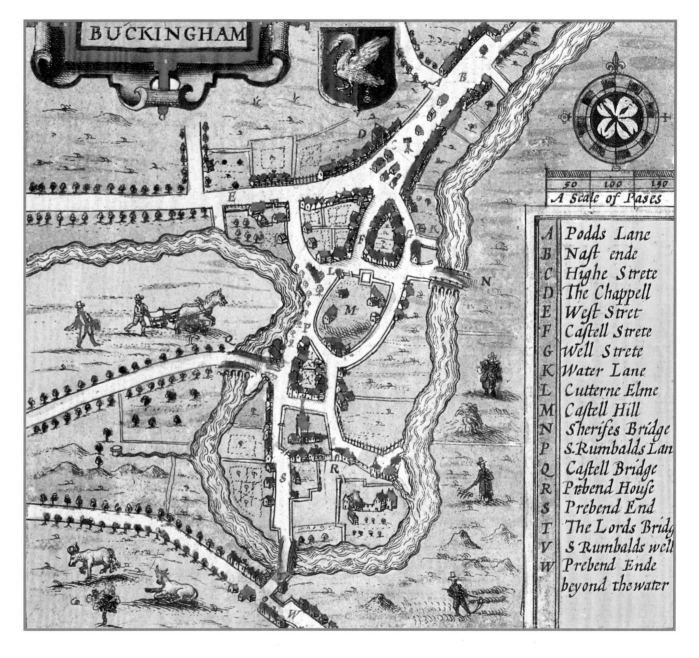

BUCKINGHAM

A Scale of Pases

50 100 150

A	Podds Lane
B	Naſt ende
C	Highe Strete
D	The Chappell
E	Weſt Stret
F	Caſtell Strete
G	Well Strete
K	Water Lane
L	Cutterne Elme
M	Caſtell Hill
N	Sherifes Bridge
P	S. Rumbalds Lan
Q	Caſtell Bridge
R	Prebend Houſe
S	Prebend End
T	The Lords Bridg
V	S Rumbalds well
W	Prebend Ende
	beyond the water

CAMBRIDGE

'From ancient Grantcester, Camboritum by Antonine, now famous Cambridge, the other breast and Nurse-mother of all pious literature, have flowed full streams of the learned Sciences into all other parts of this Land and elsewhere: ancient indeed, if their Story be rightly writ, that will have it built by Cantaber a Spaniard, three hundred seventy five years before the birth of our Saviour, who thither first brought and planted the Muses.

By their increase being straightned, the Students complain (as the Prophets did to Elisha) that the place was too little for them to dwell in, therefore inlarging more Northward, seated themselves neer unto the Bridge, whereupon the place began to be called Grant-bridge, though others from the crooked River Came will have it named Cambridge. This place (though sacred, and exempted from Mars, as Sylla once spake, when he spared Athens) the Danes in their destructions regarded no whit, wherein they often wintred after their spoils, and left the scars of their savage sores ever behind them. And in the year 1010, when Sven in his fierceness bare down all before him, this place was no place for Scholars to be in: Wars loud alarums ill consorting the Muses mild harmonies. Yet when the Normans had got the Garland on their heads, and these Danish storms turned into sun-shine daies, Gislebert the Monk, with Odo, Terricus, and William, all three of the like Monastical Profession, in the Raign of King Henry the first, resorted unto this place, and in a public Barn read the Lectures of Grammar, Logick, and Rhetorick, and Gislebert Divinity upon the Sabbath and Festival daies. From this little fountain (sayeth Peter Blessensis) grew a great River, which made all England fruitful, by the many Masters and Teachers proceeding out of Cambridge as out of a holy Paradise of God. The first Colledge therein endowed with Possessions was Peter-house, built by Hugh Balsham Bishop of Ely in the year of Grace, 1284, whose godly example many others fol-lowed; so that at this day there are sixteen most stately Colledges and Halls, for building, beauty, endowments, and store of students, so replenished, that unless it be in her other Sister Oxford, the like are not found in all Europe. But at what time it was made an University, let Robert de Remyngton tell you for me. In the Raign (sayeth he) of King Edward the first, Grantbridge, of a School, by the Court of Rome, was made an University, such as Oxford is. Lastly, the Meridian line cutting the Zenith over this City is measured from the furthest West-point according to Mercator, 20 degrees, 50 scruples, and the Arch of the same Meridian lying between the Aequator and Vertical-point is 52 degrees, 20 scruples.'

❧

¶ Speed's map of Cambridgeshire is acknowledged to be one of his finest, not least for the decorative border of the coats of arms of all the colleges. His affection and admiration for the University shows clearly in his description, and the plan, though not based on his own survey but that of John Hamond in 1592, has scroll-work incorporated into the right-hand border to provide additional appeal. Note the name just above Kings College, shown as 'Kinges colledge backesides'.

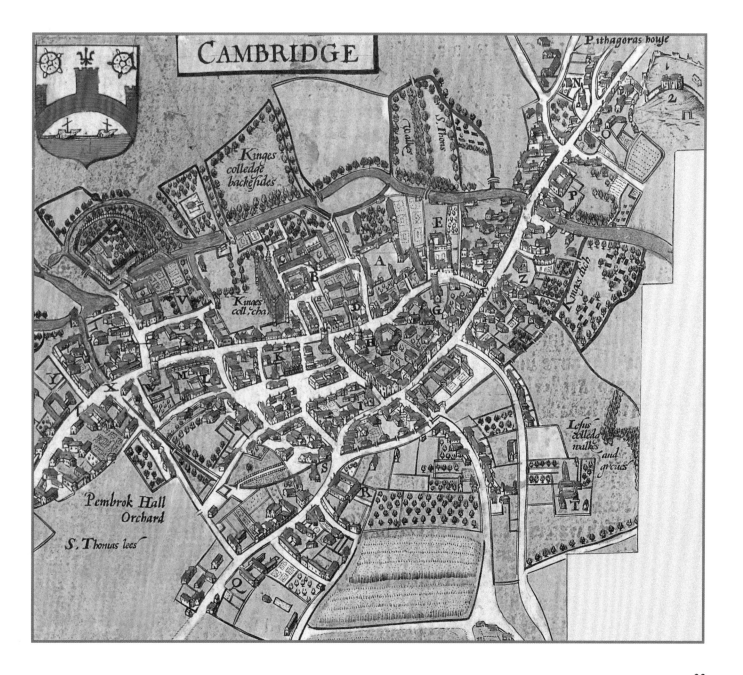

CANTERBURY

'Kent is enriched with 2 Cities and Bishops Sees, strengthened with 27 Castles, graced with 8 of his Majesty most Princely Houses, traded with 32 Market towns, and beautified with many stately and gorgeous Buildings. The chiefest City thereof, the Metropolitan and Archbishops See, is Canterbury, built (as our British Historians report) 900 years before the birth of Christ, by Henry of Huntington, called Caier-Kent, wherein (as M.Lambard saith) was erected the first School of professed Arts and Sciences, and the same a pattern unto Sigebert K.of East Angles, for his foundation at Cambridge: notwithstanding by the computation of time, this Sigebert was slain by Penda King of Mercia, 30 years before that Theodore the Grecian was Bishop of Canterbury who is said to be the erector of that Academy. But certain it is, that Austen the Monk had made this City famous before that time, by the conversion of these Saxons unto Christianity, and in building a most magnificent Church to Gods service,

wherein 8 of their Kings have been interred, but all their Monuments since overshadowed by the height of Beckets Tombe, that for glory, wealth, and superstitious worships equalised the Pyraminde of Aegypt or the Oracles of Delphos, yet now with Dagon is fallen before the Ark of God.

This City hath been honoured with the presence and Coronations of K.John and Queen Isabel his Wife, with the Marriages of K.Henry III. and of K.Edward I. and with the Interments of Edward the Black Prince, King Henry IV. and of Queen Joan his Wife: as Feversham is with the Burials of K.Stephen, and of Maude his Q. and Wife. But as in glory so in adversity hath this City born a part, being divers times afflicted by the Danes, but most especially in the days of King Ethelred, who in that revenge of their massacre, made havock of all, and herein slew 43200 persons, the tenth besides reserved to live. Afterward it recovered breath and beauty by the liberality of

the Bishop of Lanford; Charters and Priviledges by K.Henry III. strength in Trench and Fortifications from K.Richard II. and lastly, Walls for her defence by Simon Sudbury, Archbishop of that See: whose Graduation is placed for latitude 51.25. and parallelized for longitude 22.8. her sister Rochester differing not much in either degree.' 🦋

¶ Modern-day pilgrims and visitors alike are able to step back in time when in the centre of Canterbury. That it has changed so little since mediaeval times is our great good fortune, as is the case with many of our finest Cathedral cities. The landmarks of Speed's time are nearly all still present, and his plan corresponds remarkably with the present city centre.

	KEY				
A	West Gate	2	S. Margret str	27	S. Mary Bredin ch
B	Shaffords mill	3	S. Margret ch	28	S. Mary Bredman
C	St Peters church	4	Whitstaple mark	29	Mary Madeline
D	St Peters lane	6	High stret	30	Burgate stret
E	St Peters well	7	S.George churc	31	S. Michaels Gate
F	Hoopers mill	8	S. George Gate	32	S. Paules church
G	North gate chur	9	Dover lane	33	S. Austine Gate
H	North Gate	10	Ethelberts Tower	34	The Deanes house
I	S. Gregory stret	11	Austines Ruynes	35	The B. Pallace
K	S. Johns hospit	12	Dains Bridg	36	The Kinges Schole
L	Staple gate	13	Brod strete	37	The Grey friers
M	S. Alpohage chur	14	S. Gregorys	38	Shepshank lane
N	Christs Church	15	Duck lane	39	Castle strete
O	Breakpott lane	16	North lane	40	S. Mildred church
P	Kings bridge	17	The Prisone	41	The Castle
Q	East bridg Hosp	18	West Gate mill	42	The Session house
R	Rushe market	19	Holycroft chur	43	Winchip Gate
S	Bullstake	20	White friers	44	Riding Gate
T	Black friers	21	Bride well	45	Oate hill
V	Alsantes church	22	Stowre stret	46	S. Mary de Castro
W	S. Peters street	23	Waterlock	47	Pound lane
Y	Maiden lane	24	Iury lane	48	Maynard Spittle
X	The Mercery	25	Haukes lane	49	Pillory lane
Z	S. Andrews chu	26	Watling stret	50	Ironvarr lane

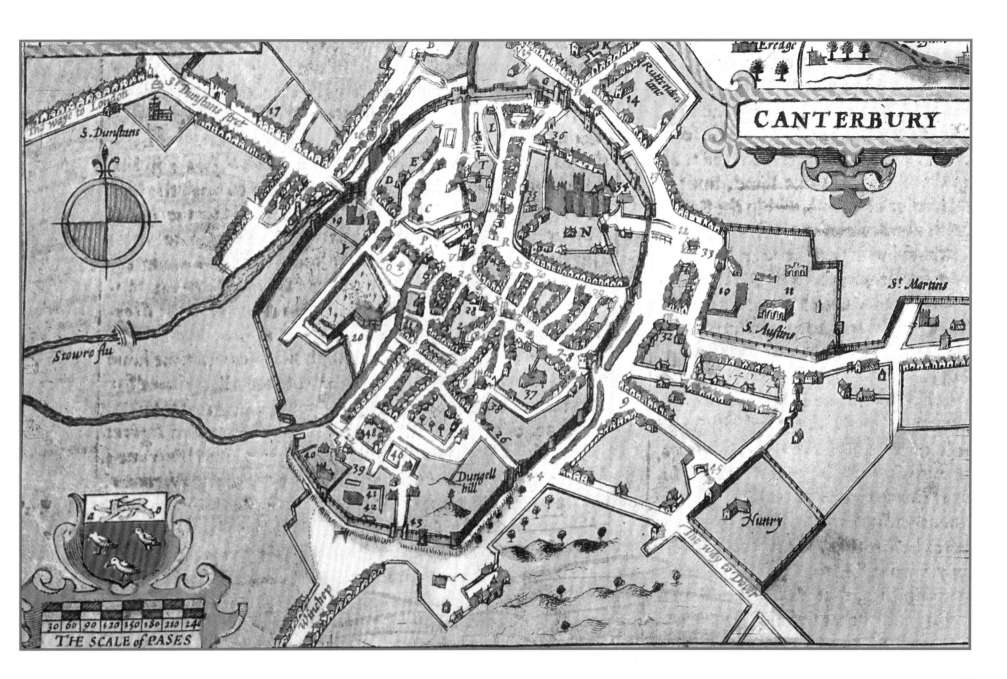

CANTERBURY

The waye to London
S. Dunstans
St Dunstans stret
Stowre flu

Rutterden lane
Eredge

St Martins
S. Austins
Nunry

Dungell hill
The way to Dover
Winchep

THE SCALE of PASES
30 60 90 120 150 180 210 240

35

CARLISLE

'The chiefest City in this Shire [Cumberland] is Carlile, pleasantly seated betwixt the Rivers Eden, Petereu, and Caud, by the Romans called Luguzallum; by Beda, Luel; by Ptolemy, Leucopibia; by Ninius, Caer-Lualid; and by us Carlile. This City flourishing under the Romans, at their departure by the furious outrages of the Scots and Picts was dejected, yet in the days of Egfrid King of Northumberland, was walled about: but again defaced by the over-running Danes, lay buried in her own ashes the space of two hundred years; upon whose ruines at length Rufus set his compassionate eye, and built there the Castle, planting a Colony of flemmings to secure the Coasts from the Scots, but upon better advisement removed them into Wales. After him, Henry his Brother and successor ordained this City for an Episcopal See: whose site is placed in the degree of Longitude from the first West part 17.and 2.scruples, and the Pole thence elevated from the degree of latitude 55.and 56.scruples.

West from hence, at Burgh upon the sand, was the fatal end of our famous Monarch King Edward the first, who there leaving his Wars unfinished against Scotland, left his troubles, and soon missed life, to his untimely and soon lamented death.

The air is piercing, and of a sharp temperature, and would be more biting, were it not that those high hills break off the Northern storms, and cold falling snows. Notwithstanding, rich is this Province, and with great varieties thereof is replenished: the hills, though rough, yet smile upon their beholders, spread with sheep and cattel the vallies stored with grass and corn sufficient: the Sea affordeth great store of fish, the land over-spread with variety of Fowls, and the rivers feed a kind of Muskle that bringeth forth Pearl, where in the mouth of the Irt as they lie gaping and sucking in dew, the Country people gather and sell to the Lapidaries, to their own little, and the buyers great gain. But the Mines Royal of Copper whereof this Country yieldeth much, is for use the richest of all: the place is at Keswick and Newland, where likewise the Black Lead is gotten, whose plenty maketh it of no great esteem; otherwise a commodity that could hardly be missed.'

¶ John Speed used available sources for town plans that were already published, and the plan of Carlisle he took from the manuscripts of his friend, the antiquary Sir Robert Cotton. The fortifications of this border town are understandably prominent at a time when there had been a constant threat from the Scots.

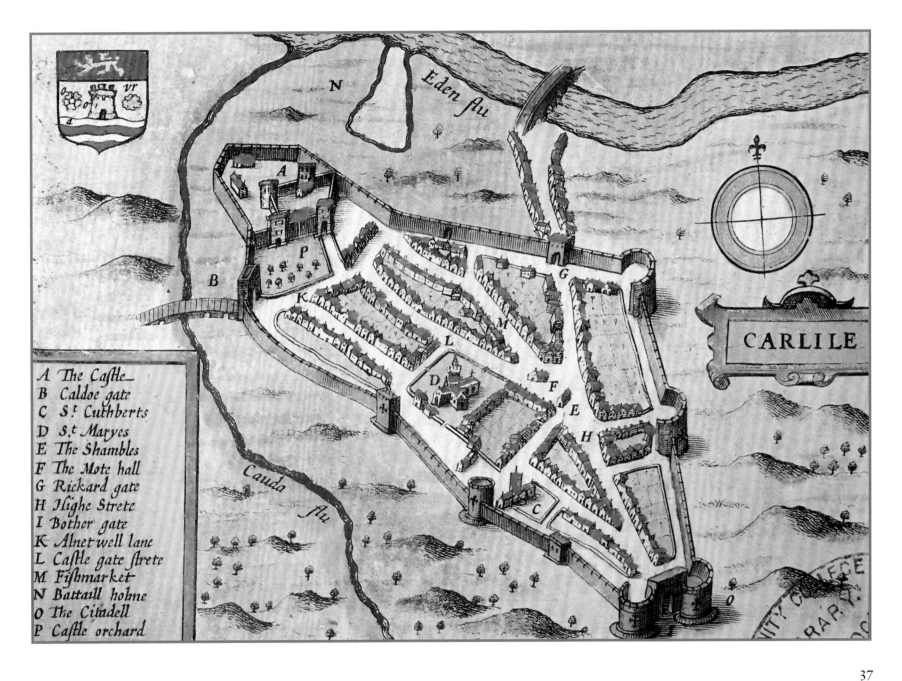

N *Eden flu*

CARLILE

Cauda flu

A The Castle
B Caldoe gate
C St Cuthberts
D St Maryes
E The Shambles
F The Mote hall
G Rickard gate
H Highe Strete
I Bother gate
K Alnet well lane
L Castle gate strete
M Fishmarket
N Battaill holme
O The Citadell
P Castle orchard

37

CHESTER

'All provision for life, are traded thorow four-teen Market-Towns in this Shire, whereof Chester is the fairest, from whom the Shire hath the name. Over Deva or Dee a fair Stone-bridge leadeth, built upon eight Arches, at either end whereof is a Gate, from whence in a long Quadren-wise the walls do encompass the City, high and strongly built, with four fair Gates opening into the four Winds besides three Posterns, and seven Watch-Towers, extending in compass 1940 paces.

On the South of this City is mounted a strong and stately Castle, round in form, and the base Court likewise inclosed with a circular wall. In the North is the Minster first built by Leofrick to the honour of S.Werburga the Virgin, and after most sumptuously repaired by Hugh the first Earl of Chester of the Normans, now the Cathedral of the Bishops See. Therein lieth interred (as report doth relate) the body of Henry the fourth, Emperor of Almane, who leaving his Imperial Estate, lead lastly therein an Hermits life.

This City hath formerly been sore defaced; first by Egfrid King of Northumberland, where he slew twelve hundred Christian Monks, resorted thither from Bangor to pray. Again by the Danes it was sore defaced, when their destroying feet had trampled down the beauty of the Land. But was again rebuilt by Edelfleada, the Mercian Lady, who in this County, and Forest of Delamer, built Eader-burg and Finborow, two fine Cities, nothing of them now remaining besides the Chamber in the Forest.

Chester in the daies of King Edgar was in most flourishing estate, wherein he had the homage of eight other Kings, who rode his Barge from S.Johns to his Palace, himself holding the Helm, as their Supream.

This City was made a County incorporate of it self by King Henry the Seventh, and is yearly governed by a Mayor, with Sword and Mace born before him in State, two Sheriffs, twenty four Aldermen, a Recorder, a Town-Clerk and a Sergeant of Peace, four Sergeants, and six Yeomen.

It hath been accounted the Key into Ireland, and great pity it is that the Port should decay as it daily doth, the Sea being stopped to scour the River by a Causey that thwarteth Dee at her bridge. Within the walls of this City are eight Parish-Churches, S.Johns the greater and lesser: in the Suburbs are the White Fryers, Black Fryers, and Nunnery now suppressed. From which City the Pole is elevated unto the degree 53,58 minutes of latitude, and from the first point of the West in longitude unto the 17th degree and 18 minutes.'

¶ The unusual shape that Speed used for this plan is attractive as an integral part of the Cheshire map, which is one of his most appealing, appropriately for his county of origin. The Roman coins illustrated were probably copied from originals in Speed's own collection.

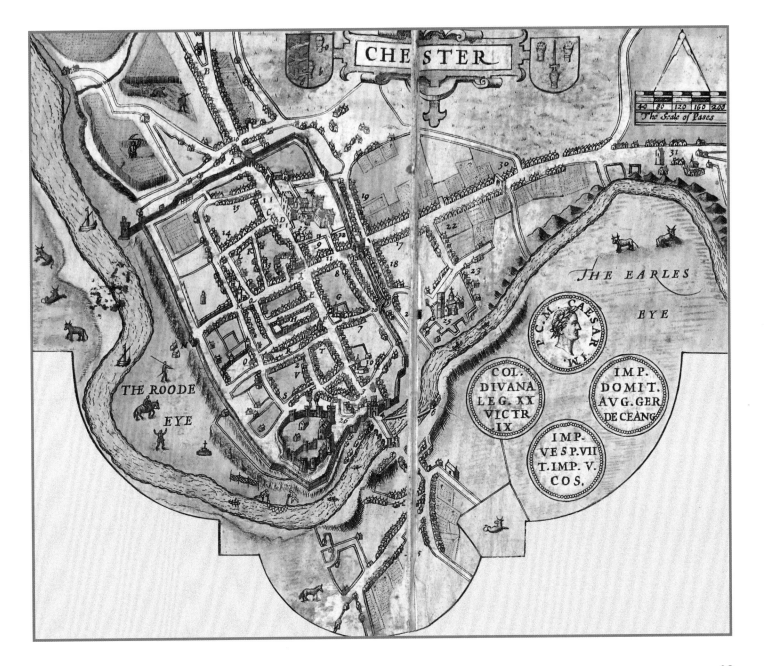

CHESTER

THE EARLES EYE

THE ROODE EYE

The Scale of Pases

P. C. M. CAESAR

COL. DIVANA LEG. XX VICTR IX

IMP. DOMIT. AVG. GER DE CEANG.

IMP. VESP. VII T. IMP. V. COS.

CHICHESTER

'The place of most account in this Shire [Sussex] is Chichester, by the Britains called Caercei, and by the Saxons Cirran Cearan, a City beautiful and large, and very well walled about, first built by Cissa the second King of the South-Saxons, wherein his Royal Palace was kept. And when K.William the first had enacted that Bishops Sees should be translated out of small Towns unto places of greater resort, the Residence of the Bishop (until then held at Selsey) was removed to this City, where Bishop Raulfe began a most goodly Cathedral Church: but before it was fully finished, by a sudden mischance of fire was quite consumed. Yet the same Bishop, with the helping Liberality of K.Henry the first, began it again, and saw it wholly finished; whose Beauty and Greatness her fatal enemy still envying, again cast down in the days of K.Rich.the first, and by her raging flames consumed the Buildings both of it and the Bishops Palace adjoyning, which Seffrid, the second Bishop of that name, reedified and built anew. And now, to augment the Honour of this place, the City hath born the Title of an Earldom; whereof they of Arundel were sometimes so stiled.

Whose Graduation for Latitude is removed from the Equator unto the degree 50.55 minutes; and for Longitude, observing the same point in the West, whence Mercator hath measured are 20 degrees.

The Air is good, though somewhat clouded with mists, which arise from off her South-bordering Sea, who is very prodigal unto her for Fish and Sea-fowl, though as sparing for Harbours or Ships arrivage, and those which she hath, as uncertain for continuance, as dangerous for entrance.

Rich is the Soil and yieldeth great plenty of all things necessary, but very ill for Travellers, especially in the winter, the Land lying low, and the Ways very deep, whose middle tract is garnished with Meadows, Pastures and Corn-fields: the Sea-coast with Hills which are called the Downs, abundantly yielding Grain and Grass.'

¶ The simple cruciform layout of central Chichester is as apparent today as in Speed's time, and there is still much evidence of the mediaeval city walls. The plan has no scale shown and Speed did not claim authorship, having taken both the map of Sussex and the plan of Chichester from John Norden's publication of 1599, which Speed acknowledges on his map.

KEY

A	S. Martynes	M	Crandane
B	The Pallant	N	West lane
C	Pallant street	O	St Toolies
D	Blackfryers	P	S. Richards min
E	S. Andrews	Q	Our Laydyes chap.
F	S. Maryes Hospt.	R	East Gate
G	Greyfryers	S	S. Pancras
H	The Pallace	T	S. Bartholme
I	S. Peters	V	S. quitry Bridg
K	Paradice	W	South Gate
L	East lane	X	North Gate

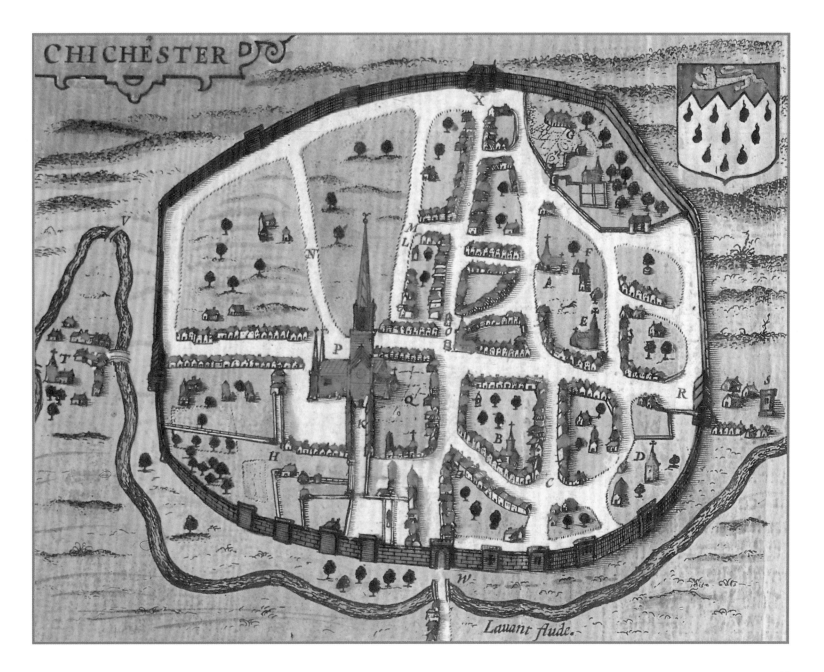

CHICHESTER

Lauant flude.

COLCHESTER

'The chiefest City for account at this day, in this Shire [Essex], is Colchester, built by Coilus the British Prince 124 years after the birth of our Saviour Christ, (if he of Monmouth say true) wherein his son Lucius, Helena, and Constan-tine, the first Christian King, Empress, and Emperor in the World were born: which made Necham for Constantine to sing as he did.

> From Colchester there rose a Star,
> The rayes whereof gave glorious light
> Throughout the World in Climates far,
> Great Constantine, Rome's Emperor bright.

And the Romans to the great honour of Helena, inscribed her, Piissima Venerabilis Augusta. But of these we shall be occasioned to speak more hereafter. This City is situated upon the South of the River Coln; from whence it has the name, and is walled about, raised upon an high trench of earth, though now much decayed, having six gates of entrance, and three posterns in the West-wall, besides nine Watch-towers for defence, and containeth in compass 1980 paces; wherein stand eight fair churches and two other without the walls, for Gods divine service; S.Tenants and the Black Fryers decayed in the suburbs; Mary Magdelens, the Nunnery, S.Johns, and the Crouched Fryers, all suppressed: within towards the East is mounted an old Castle, and elder ruines upon a trench containing two acres of ground, where as yet may be seen the provident care they had against all ensuing assaults. The trade of this Town standeth chiefly in making of Cloth and Baies, with Sayes, and other like Stuffs daily invented; and is governed by two Bailiffs, twelve Aldermen, all wearing Scarlet; a Recorder, a Town-clerk and four Sergeants at Mace. Whose position for latitude is in the degree 52,14 minutes; and for longitude, in the degree 21, and 50 minutes.

The air is temperate and pleasant, only towards the waters somewhat aguish; the soil is rich and fruitful, though in some place sandy and barren; yet so that it never frustrates the Husbandmans hopes, or fills not the hands of her harvest Labourers: but in some part so fertile, that after three years glebe of Saffron, the Land for 18 more will yield plenty of Barly, without either dung or other fatning earth.'

❡ A typical town plan by John Speed; clear, well balanced and elegant. The 20th century claim by Colchester to be Britain's oldest town is based on more recent discoveries which indicate a town there in the 1st century BC, and a settlement as much as nine centuries earlier.

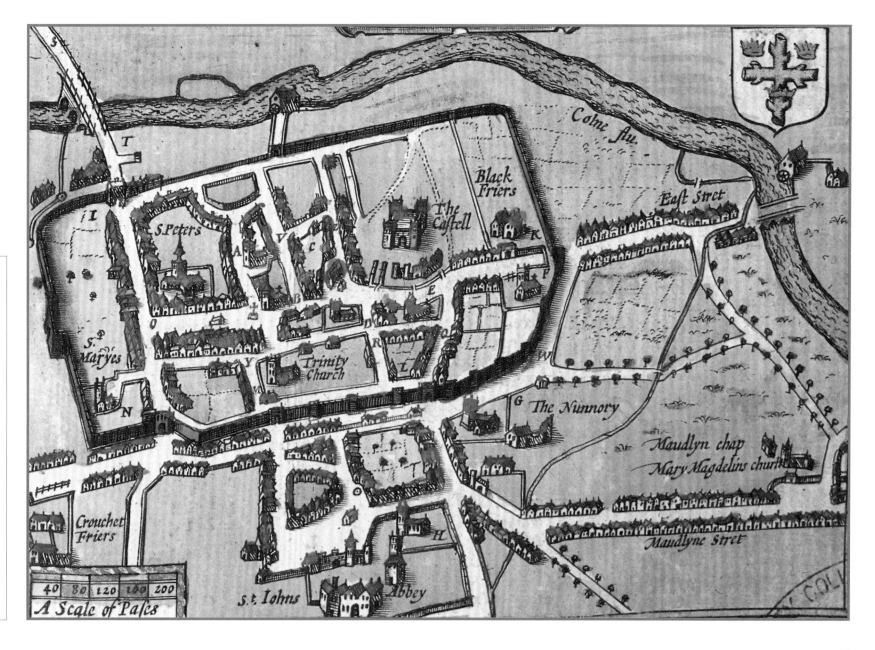

KEY

A. S. Martins
B. S. Rumbals
C. S. Tenants chap.
D. S. Nicolas
E. Halhalowes
F. S. Iames
G. S. Bothals
H. S. Gylles
I. North Gate
K. East Gate
L. Bothals Gate
M. Shire Gate
N. Head Gate
O. Highe Stret
P. East Stret
Q. Bothals Stret
R. Wye Stret
S. Cowe Stret
T. Midlehorow
V. Bouchers
W. More elm lane
X. Trinity lane
Y. S. Martins lane
Z. Tenants lane

Colne flu.

Black Friers

The Castell

East Stret

S. Peters

S. Maryes

Trinity Church

The Nunnory

Maudlyn chap
Mary Magdelins church

Crouchet Friers

Maudlyne Stret

A Scale of Paces
40 80 120 160 200

St. Iohns Abbey

43

COVENTRY

'Surely, by the testimony of John Rosse and others, this County [Warwickshire] hath been better replenished with people, who maketh complaint of whole townships depopulations, altogether laid waste by a puissant Army of feeding Sheep. Notwithstanding, many fair Towns it hath, and some of them matchable to the most of England. The chief thereof is Coventry, a City both for stately building and walled for defence: whose citizens having highly offended their first Lord Leofrick, had their priviledges infringed, and themselves oppressed with many heavy Tributes; whose wife Lady Godiva pitying their estates, uncessantly sued for their peace, and that with such importunacy, as hardly could be said whether was greater, his hatred, or her love; at last overcome with her continual intercessions, he granted her suit, upon an uncivil, and (as he thought) an unacceptable condition, which was, that she should ride naked thorow the face of the City and that openly at high noon-day. This notwithstanding she thankfully accepted, and performed the act accordingly enjoyned: for this Lady Godiva stripping herself of all rich atire, let loose the tresses of her fair hair, which on every side so covered her nakedness, that no part of her body was uncivil to sight; whereby she redeemed the former freedoms, and remission of such heavy Tributes. Whose memory I wish may remain honourable in that City forever, and her pitty [piety] followed by such possessing Ladies.

This City had grant to chuse their yearly Magistrates, a Major and two Bailiffs, and to build about and embattle a wall by K.Edward the third, whom Henry the sixth, corporated a County of itself, and changed the names of their Bailiffs unto Sheriffs; and the walls then were built as they now stand, thorow which open 13 Gates for entrance, besides 18 other Towers thereon for defence.

At Gofford gate in the East hangeth the shield-bone of a Wild Boar, (or rather an Elephant being not so little as a yard in length) far bigger then the greatest Ox-bone: with whose snout the great pit called Swanswell was turned up, and was slain by the famous Guy, if we will believe report.'

¶ It is not surprising that this plan omits any representation of Lady Godiva, for John Speed was very correct in his approach, and his references to her in his description indicate appropriate respect. The city plan, not his own, has a huge number of streets and buildings identified and gives a clear indication of Coventry's importance 400 years ago.

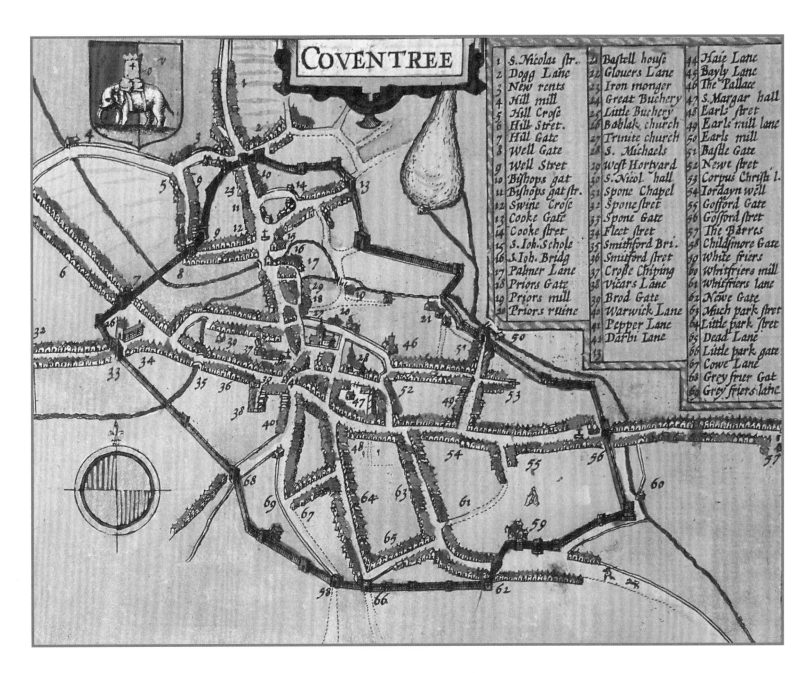

COVENTREE

1 S. Nicolas str.	21 Bastell house	44 Haie Lane
2 Dogg Lane	22 Glouers Lane	45 Bayly Lane
3 New rents	23 Iron monger	46 The Pallace
4 Hill mill	24 Great Buchery	47 S. Margar hall
5 Hill Crose	25 Little Buchery	48 Earls stret
6 Hill Stret.	26 Bablak church	49 Earls mill lane
7 Hill Gate	27 Trinite church	50 Earls mill
8 Well Gate	28 S. Michaels	51 Bastle Gate
9 Well Stret	29 West Hortyard	52 Newe stret
10 Bishops gat	30 S. Nicol. hall	53 Corpus Christi l.
11 Bishops gat str.	31 Spone Chapel	54 Iordayn well
12 Swine Crose	32 Spone stret	55 Gosford Gate
13 Cooke Gate	33 Spone Gate	56 Gosford stret
14 Cooke stret	34 Fleet stret	57 The Barres
15 S. Ioh. Schole	35 Smithsford Bri.	58 Childsmore Gate
16 S. Ioh. Bridg	36 Smitford stret	59 White friers
17 Palmer Lane	37 Crose Chiping	60 Whitfriers mill
18 Priors Gate	38 Vicars Lane	61 Whitfriers lane
19 Priors mill	39 Brod Gate	62 Newe Gate
20 Priors ruine	40 Warwick Lane	63 Much park stret
	41 Pepper Lane	64 Little park stret
	42 Darbi Lane	65 Dead Lane
		66 Little park gate
		67 Cowe Lane
		68 Grey frier Gat
		69 Grey friers lane

DERBY

'Places for commerce, or memorable note, the first is Darby, the Shire-town called by the Danes Deorby, seated upon the West bank of Derwent, where also a small Brook rising Westward, runneth thorow the Town under nine Bridges, before it meets with her far greater River Derwent, which presently it doth, after she hath passed Tenant Bridge in the South-east of the Town. But a Bridge of more beauty, built all of Free-stone, is passed over Derwent in the North-east of the Town, whereon standeth a fair stone Chapell, and both of them bearing the names of Saint Maries: five other Churches are in this Town, the chiefest whereof is called Alhallowes, whose Steeple or Bell-Tower being both beautiful and high, was built onely at the charges of young men and maids, as is witnessed by the inscription cut in the same upon every square of the Steeple.

Among the miserable desolations of the Danes, this Town bare a part, but by Lady Ethelfleda was again repaired, and is at this day incorporated with the yearly government of two Bailiffs Elect, out of twenty four brethren, besides as many Burgesses of Common Counsel, a Recorder, Town-clerk, and two Sergeants with Mace: whose Graduation is observed from the Equator to be 53 degrees, 25 scruples, and from the first point in the West, 19 degrees, 2 scruples.

Derbyshire is stored with many commodities, and them of much worth; for besides woods and cattle, sheep and corn, every where over-spreading the face of this County, the Mill-stone, Crystal, and Allablaster, the Mines of Pit-coal, and Lead, are of great price: whereof the last is mentioned in Pliny, who writeth that in Brittain, in the very crust of the ground, without any deep digging, is gotten so great store of Lead, that there is a Law expresly made of purpose, forbidding men to make more then to a certain stint. Whose stones are plenteously gotten in those Mountains, and melted into Sowes, to no small profit of the Country. There is also in certain veins of the earth, Stibium, which the Apothecaries call Antimonium, and the Alchymists hold it in great esteem.'

¶ The compass rose on this plan, whilst not decorative by cartographic standards of the time, is better than many used on the plans. The elaborate and striking compass roses which feature on some of the county maps are by contrast almost works of art in themselves. The river shown as Darwen is the Derwent.

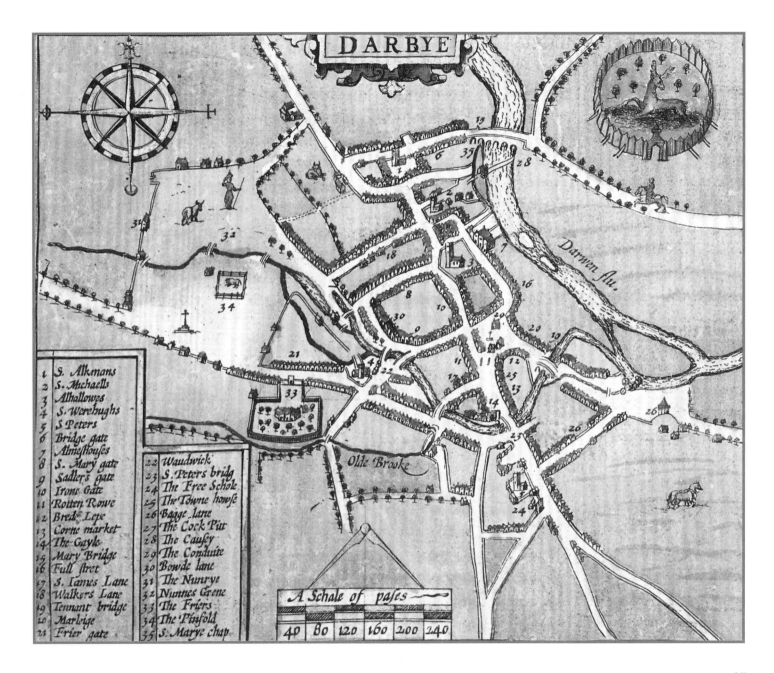

DARBYE

Darwen flu.

Olde Brooke

1	S. Alkmans
2	S. Michaells
3	Alhallowes
4	S. Werehughs
5	S. Peters
6	Bridge gate
7	Almeshouses
8	S. Mary gate
9	Sadler's gate
10	Irone Gate
11	Rotten Rowe
12	Bredr. Lepe
13	Corne market
14	The Gayle
15	Mary Bridge
16	Full stret
17	S. Iames Lane
18	Walkers Lane
19	Tennant bridge
20	Marloige
21	Frier gate

22	Waudwick
23	S. Peters bridg
24	The Free Schole
25	The Towne howse
26	Bagge lane
27	The Cock Pitt
28	The Causey
29	The Conduite
30	Bowde lane
31	The Nunrye
32	Nunnes Greene
33	The Friers
34	The Pinsfold
35	S. Marye chap.

A Schale of pases

40	80	120	160	200	240

47

DORCHESTER

'Commodities arising in this Country [county – ie Dorset] are chiefly Wools and Woods in her North, where the Forests are stored with the one, and the pleasant green Hills with the other. The inner part is overspread both with corn and grass, and the Sea yieldeth the Isidis Plocamos, a shrub growing not unlike the Coral, without any leaf; besides her other gifts, turning all to great gain: which the more is made manifest by the many Market-Towns in this Shire, whereof Dorcester is the chief, in Antonius his Itinerarium termed Durnovaria, situated upon the South side of Frome, and the Roman Causey called Fossway, wherein some of their Legions kept, as by the Rampiers and Coins there daily digged up, is probably conjectured; at which time it seemeth the City was walled, whereof some part yet standeth, especially upon the West and South sides, and the Tract and Trench most apparent in a Quadrant-wise almost meeteth the River, containing in circuit one thousand and seven hundred paces, but were cast down by the Danes, whose trampling feet destroyed all things wheresoever they came, and hands here razed the Trenches Maudbury and Poundbury, the seals of their siege, and signs of times misery. About three hundred paces Southward from hence standeth an old fortification of Earth trenched about, and mounted above the ordinary plain thirty paces, containing some five acres of ground, wherein (at my there-being) plenty of Corn grew. This the Inhabitants call The Maiden Castle, having entrance thereunto only upon the East and West. This is thought to have been a Summer-Camp or Station of the Romans, when their Garrisons kept the frontiers of this Province.

The Government of this City is yearly committed to two bayliffs, elected out of eight Magistrates or Aldermen, a Recorder, Town-Clerk, and two Sergeants attending them: whence the North-pole is elevated 50 degrees, 48 minutes in latitude, and for longitude is removed from the first West point unto the Meridian of 18 degrees.

The Air is good, and of an healthful constitution: the Soil is fat, affording many commodities, and the Countrey most pleasant in her situation: for the In-land is watred with many sweet and fresh running springs, which taking passage thorow the plain Valleys, do lastly in a loving manner unite themselves together, and of their many branches make many big bodied streams: neither doth the Sea deny them entrance, but helpeth rather to fill up their banks, whereby Vessels of burden discharge their rich treasures, and her self with open hand distributeth her gifts all along the South of this Shore.'

¶ This rather simple plan by Speed has no key of letters or numbers to identify streets and buildings, although a few names are engraved directly on the plan. Much of today's town was rebuilt in the 17th and 18th centuries to repair fire damage, but the main streets conform closely to those shown here.

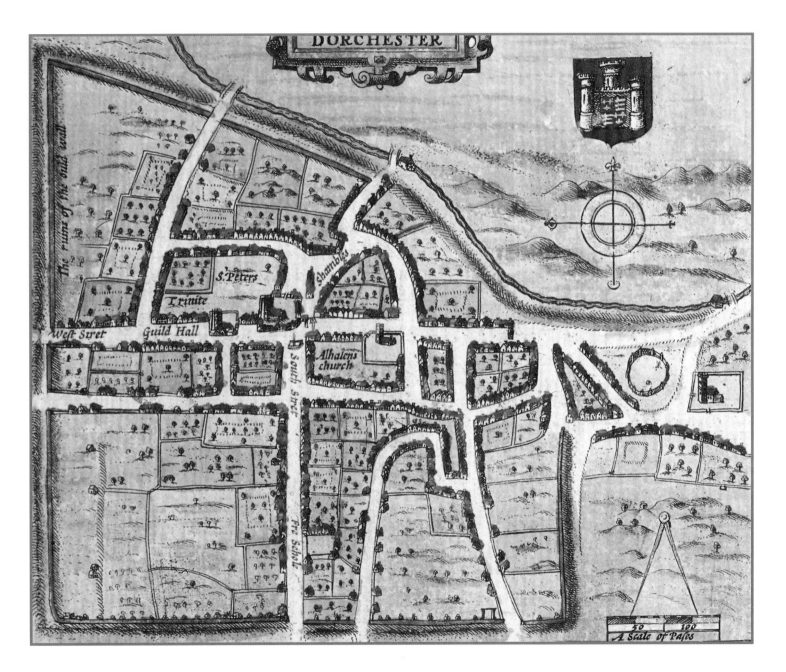

DORCHESTER

The ruins of the ould wall

S. Peters

Shambles

Trinite

West Stret   Guild Hall

Alhalens church

South Stret

Fre Schole

50   100
A Scale of Paſes

49

DURHAM

'Over this County, the Bishops thereof have had the Royalties of Princes, and the Inhabitants have pleaded priviledge not to pass in service of war over the River of Tees or Tyne; whose charge (as they have alledged) was to keep and defend the corpse of S.Cuthbert their great and adored Saint, and therefor they termed themselves, The Holy-werk-folks. And the repute of this Cuthbert and his supposed defence against the Scots was such, that our English Kings in great devotion have gone in pilgrimage to visit his Tomb, and have given many large possessions to his Church: such were King Egfrid, Aelsred, and Guthrun the Dane, Edward, and Athelstan Monarch of England, and zealous Canute, the greatest of all, who came thither barefooted, and at Cuthberts Tomb both augmented and confirmed their Liberties. This Saint then, of nothing made Durham become great, and Will.the Conquerour, of a Bishoprick made it a County Palatine: at that time William Careleph, Bishop of the Diocess pulled down the old Church which Aldwin

had built, and with sumptuous cost laid the foundations of a new, wherein St.Cuthbert's Shrine in the vacancy of the Bishops was the Keeper of the Castle-Keyes.

In the West of this Church, and place called Gallile, the Marble Tomb of Venerable Beda remaineth, who was born at Iarro in this County, and became a Monk at Weremouth, whose painful industries and light of learning in those times of darkness are wonderful, as the volumes which he wrote do well declare. And had the idol Monks of England imployed their times after his example, their Founders expectations had not been frustrate, nor those foundations so easily overturned. But the revenge of sin ever following the actions of sins, dissolved first the largenesses of this Countys small liberties, under the reign of King Edward the first, and since hath shaken to pieces those places herein erected, under the Reign of K.Henry the eight: such were Durham, Sherborn, Stayndrop, Iarro, Weremouth, and

Egleton, all which felt the reward of their idleness, and wrath of him that is jealous of his own honour.

The air is sharp and very piercing, and would be more, were it not that the vapours from the German-Seas did help much to dissolve her ice and snow: and the store of coals therein growing and gotten, do warm the body, and keep back the cold, which fuel, besides their own use, doth yield great commodities unto this Province by trade thereof into other parts.'

¶ Apart from London and Westminster, this is the only English plan in Speed's atlas to omit a key or any engraved names of locations. The descriptive panel, transcribed opposite, gives no identity to the main landmarks, except the castle. The cathedral is sufficiently well shown to be self-evident, but otherwise it might be assumed that the plan by Matthew Patteson of 1595 from which Speed copied, was lacking in detail.

'The ancient Citie Duram, by the Saxons called Dunholm, which as Beda sayth is compounded of their two words Dun, an hill & Holm an Island, is in like forme and sittuation as here is described. The first erectors of this Citie are sayde to be the Monkes of Lindisferne which by the raging of the Danes were drivn thence, and wandring farre and wyde, at last by oracle (as in those dayes there were maney, yf we will beleve their monkish legende) they were comanded to seat here, about the yere of grace 995, where Cuthbert their Bishop obtayned a great opinion of Santitye and no lesse revenews, and authoritye.

  In the upper part of this Citie, mounted upon an hill, William the Conqueror, for her defence built a strong Castell; and for her profitt and pleasure, nature hath girtt her almost round, with ye sweet and delectable ryver of were.'

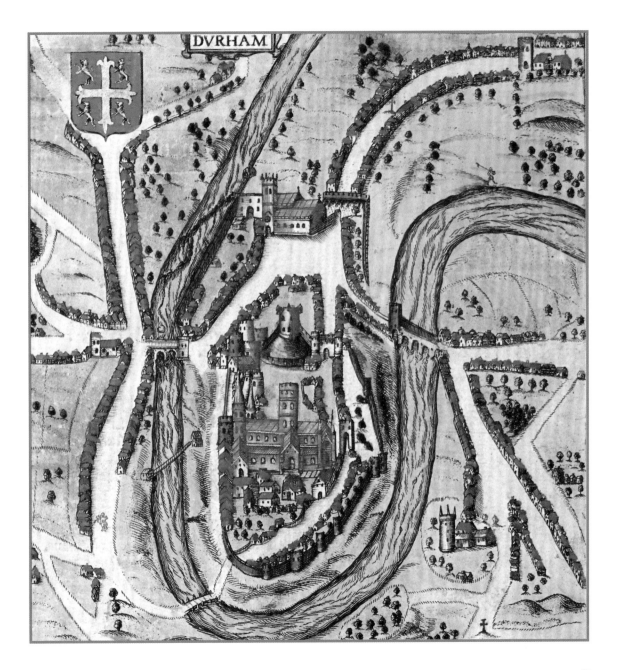

 (label within image: DVRHAM)

ELY

'Another City formerly in great fame is Ely, by the Saxons Elig, had in account for the repute and holiness of Votary Nunns their residing; built first by Audrey, wife to one Tombert a Prince in this Province who had this place as a part of her Dowry: she having departed from her second husband Egbert, King of Northumberland, devoted her self to the service of God, and built here a Monastery, whereof she became the first Abbess. This in the Danish desolations was destroyed, but soon after reedified by Ethelwold Bishop of Winchester, who stored it with Monks; unto whom King Edgar granted the jurisdiction over four hundreds and an half, within these Fenns and the East-angles limits, which to this day are called The Liberties of S.Audrey: after whose examples many Nobles so enriched it with large Revenues, that as Malmesbury saith the Abbot thereof laid up yearly in his Coffers a thousand and four hundred pounds. And of latter times the Monks thereof became so wealthy, that

their old decayed Church they renewed with new and most stately buildings, which is now the Cathedral of the Diocess, and for beauty giveth place to no other in the Land. Eight other foundations set apart from secular use in this Province were at Thorney, Charteres, Denny, Elsey, Beach, Barnwel, Swasey and Shengey, all which in the daies of King Henry the Eighth came to the period of their surpassing wealth, and left there Lands to the dispose of his Will.

This Province [Cambridgeshire] is not large, nor for air greatly to be liked, having the Fenns so spread upon her North, that they infect the air far into the rest: from whose furthest point unto Roiston in the South are thirty five miles; but in the broadest is not fully twenty: the whole in circumference, traced by the compass of her many indents, one hundred twenty and eight miles.

The soil doth differ both in air and commodities; the Fenny surcharged with waters: the South is Champion, and yieldeth Corn in abundance,

with Meadowing-pastures upon both sides of the River Came, which divides that part of the Shire in the midst, upon whose East-bank the Muses have built their most sacred Seat where with plenteous increase they have continued for these many hundred years.'

¶ This plan has many of the quaint features that were typical of Speed's draughtsmanship, and the depiction of hunters in the fields, nearly as tall as the Cathedral, only increases its charm. The sugar-loaf hills are hard to find in the Fens, but certainly make the windmills more attractive and prominent.

The inclusion of Ely in the map of Huntingdonshire is another example of Speed's flexibility in his compilation, as in a number of other cases, and he always turns necessity to advantage by providing additional decorative panels to explain these apparently wrong locations.

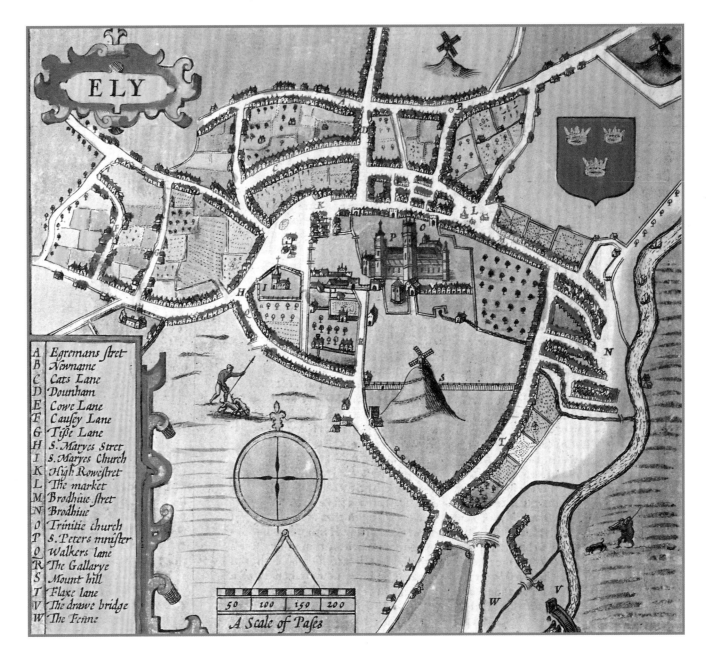

A	Egremans stret
B	Newname
C	Cats Lane
D	Dounham
E	Cowe Lane
F	Causey Lane
G	Tisse Lane
H	S. Maryes Stret
I	S. Maryes Church
K	High Rowestret
L	The market
M	Brodhiue stret
N	Brodhiue
O	Trinitie church
P	S. Peters minster
Q	Walkers lane
R	The Gallarye
S	Mount hill
T	Flaxe lane
V	The drawe bridge
W	The Fenne

ELY

50	100	150	200

A Scale of Pases

EXETER

'Excester the chief City and Shire-Town of this County [Devon] is seated on that River [Exe] and pleasantly upon the gentle ascent of an hill, so stately for building so rich with Inhabitants, so frequent for commerce and concourse of strangers, that a man can desire nothing but there it is to be had, saith William of Malmesbury. The walls of this City first built by King Athelstan, are in a manner circular or round, but towards the Ex rangeth almost in a straight line, having six Gates for entrance, and many watch-towers interposed betwixt, whose compass containeth about fifteen hundred paces: upon the East part of this City standeth a Castle called Rugemont, sometimes the Palace of the West Saxon Kings, and after them of the Earls of Cornwal, whose prospect is pleasant unto the Sea, and over against it a most magnificent Cathedral Church, founded by King Athelstan also, in honour of St.Peter, and by Edward the Confessor made the Bishops See, which he removed from Crediton or Kirton in this County, unto the City of Excester, (as saith

the private History of that place:) whose delapidations the Reverend Father in God, William, now Bishop of the Diocess, with great cost hath repaired; whom I may not name without a most thankful remembrance for the great benefits received by his careful providence toward me and mine.

This City was so strong, and so well stored of Britains, that they held out against the Saxons for 465 years after their first entrance, and was not absolutely won until Athelstan became Monarch of the whole, who then peopled it with his Saxons, and enriched the beauty thereof with many fair buildings: but in the times of the Danish desolations this City with the rest felt their destroying hands; for in the year 875 it was by them sore afflicted, spoiled, and shaken, and that most grivously by Swane in the year of Christ Jesus 1003, who razed it down from East to West, so that scarcely had it gotton breath before William the Bastard of Normandy besieged it, against whom the Citizens with great

manhood served, till a part of the wall fell down of it self, and that by the hand of God's providence, saith mine Author: since when it hath been three times besieged, and with valiant resistance ever defended. The first was by Hugh Courtney Earl of Devonshire, in the civil broils betwixt Lancaster and York; then by Perkin Warbeck, that counterfeited Richard Duke of York; and lastly, by the Cornish Rebels, wherein although the Citizens were grievously pinched with scarcity, yet continued they their faithful allegiance unto King Edward the sixth and at this day flourisheth in tranquillity and wealth, being governed by a Maior, twenty four Brethren, with a Recorder, Town-Clerk, and other Officers their attendants. This Cities graduation is set in the degree of latitude from the North-pole 50, and 45 scruples: and for longitude from the West to the degree 16, and 25 scruples.' ❧

❡ A detailed plan but not by Speed. He used the fine plan that had been published a few years earlier (1587) by Hogenburg on his Devonshire map. The rather different appearance of this plan and its lettering is due to the Devonshire map probably having been engraved not by Jodocus Hondius (engraver of most of the atlas) but by another hand. Some of the copperplates were engraved by Renold Elstrack and it is probable that Devonshire was his work as well.

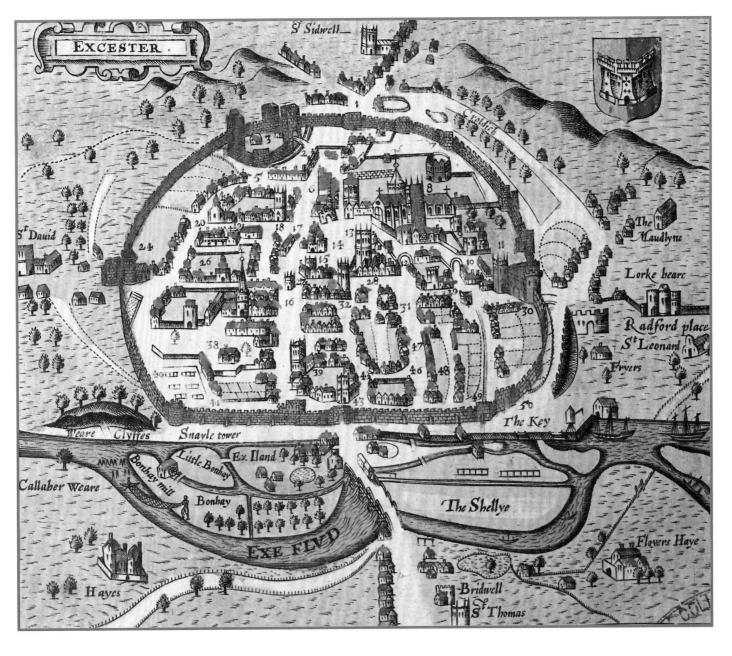

Places of the Citie by Fygures observed

1	East gate	25	Northgate stret
2	St Laurence	26	St Kerians
3	The Castle	27	Cooke rowe
4	Corrylane	28	Bell hill
5	St Iane crosse	29	Southgat stret
6	St Stephens	30	Southgate
7	Bedforde house	31	Genny stret
8	St Peters	32	St Gregories
9	Bishops pallace	33	Milklane
10	Pallace gate	34	The Shambles
11	Trinitye	35	St Olaues
12	Beare gate	36	St Mary arche
13	St Maryes	37	Arches lane
14	Churchyard	38	St Nicholas
15	St Petrokes	39	St Iohns
16	Highe strete	40	Fryer haye
17	Guild hall	41	Little Britaine
18	Alhallowes	42	Alhallowes
19	Goldsmith stret	43	St Maries steps
20	St Paule	44	West Gate
21	Paule stret	45	Smithen stret
22	St Pancras	46	Idle lane
23	Waterbery stret	47	Prestern stret
24	North gate	48	Racke lane

GLOUCESTER

'The general Commodities of this Shire are Corn, Iron, and Woolls, all passing fine; besides Pasturage, Fruits and Woods, which last are much lessened by making of Iron, the only bane of Oake, Elme, and Beech.

These, with all other provisions, are traded thorow twenty five Market-towns in this County, whereof two are Cities of no small import: the first is Glocester, from whom the Shire taketh name, seated upon Severn, neer the midst of this Shire, by Antonine the Emperor called Gleuum, built first by the Romans, and set as it were upon the neck of the Silurs to yoke them, where their Legion called Colonia Gleuum lay. It hath been walled about (excepting that part that is defended by the River) the ruines whereof in many places appear; and some part yet standing doth well witness their strength. This City was first won from the Britains by Cheulin the first King of the West-saxons, about the year of Christ 570, and afterwards under the Mercians it flourished with great honour where Osrik King of Northumberland, by the sufferance of Ethelred of Mercia, founded a most stately Monastery of Nunns, whereof Kineburgh, Eadburgh, and Eve, Queens of the Mercians, were Prioresses successively each after other.

Edelfled a most renowned Lady, Sister to King Edward the elder, in this City built a fair Church, wherein her self was interred, which being overthrown by the Danes, was afterwards rebuilt and made the Cathedral of that See, dedicated unto the honour of S.Peter. In this Church the unfortunate Prince King Edward the Second, under a Monument of Alablaster, doth lie, who being murdered at Barkley Castle by the cruelty of French Isabel his Wife, was there intombed. And not far from him another Prince as unfortunate, namely Robert Curthose, the eldest Son of William the Conqueror, lieth in a painted wooden Tomb in the midst of the Quire; whose eyes were pluck'd out in Cardiff Castle, wherein he was kept prisoner twenty six years, with all contumelious indignities, until through extreme anguish he ended his life. And before any of these, in this City, say our British Historians, the body of Lucius our first Christian King was interred: and before his days the Britains Arviragus.

The graduation of this County I observe from this City, whence the Pole is elevated in the degree of latitude 52, and 14 minutes; and in longitude from the West 18, and 5 min.'

❡ Another of the plans for which Speed does not claim authorship, though it forms an essential part of the splendid map of the county. Unusually, the map includes on the engraved surface some detail of both the cities of Bristol and Gloucester.

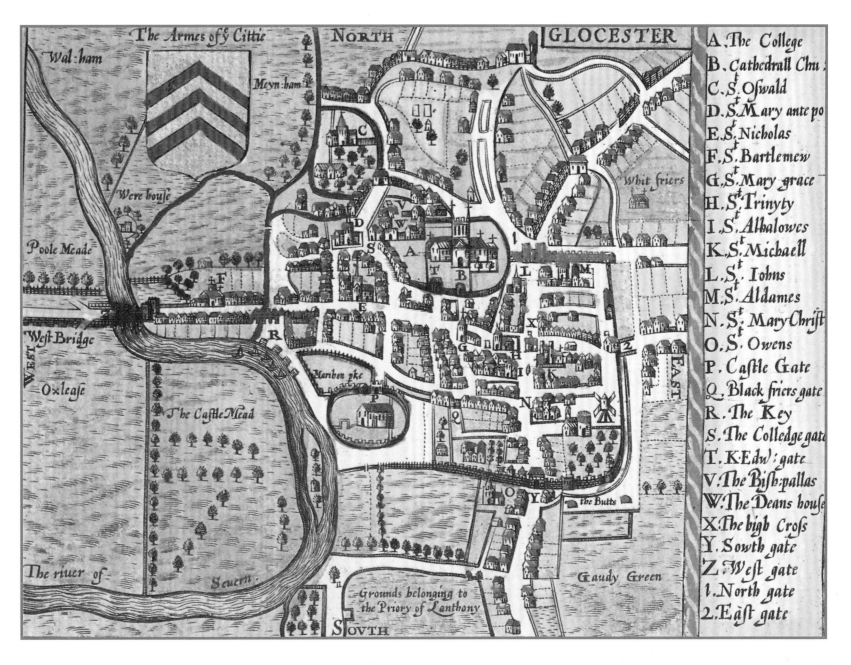

The Armes of ye Cittie   NORTH   GLOCESTER

Wal:ham
Meyn:ham

Were house
Poole Meade

West Bridge
Oxleafe

The river of Severn
The Caftle Mead

Maribon pke

WEST

Whit friers

the Butts
Gaudy Green

EAST

Grounds belonging to
the Priory of Lanthony

SOVTH

A. The College
B. Cathedrall Chu...
C. Sᵗ Oſwald
D. Sᵗ Mary ante po...
E. Sᵗ Nicholas
F. Sᵗ Bartlemew
G. Sᵗ Mary grace
H. Sᵗ Trinyty
I. Sᵗ Alhalowes
K. Sᵗ Michaell
L. Sᵗ Iohns
M. Sᵗ Aldames
N. Sᵗ Mary Chrift...
O. S. Owens
P. Caftle Gate
Q. Black friers gate
R. The Key
S. The Colledge gate
T. K Edw: gate
V. The Biſh:pallas
W. The Deans houfe
X. The high Croſs
Y. Sowth gate
Z. Weft gate
1. North gate
2. Eaſt gate

57

HEREFORD

'Raised of the ruines of old Ariconium, (now Ken-chester, shaken in pieces by a violent earth-quake) Hereford grew to great fame, through a conceived sanctity by the burial of Ethelbert King of the East-Angles, slain at Sutton by Offa, at what time he came thither to have espoused his Daughter; whose grave was first made at Marden, but afterwards canonized, and removed to this City, when in honour of him was built the Cathedral Church by Milfrid a petty King of that Country, which Gruffith Prince of South-Wales, and Algar an Englishman, rebelling against King Edward Confessor, consumed with fire; but by Bishop Reinelin was restored as now it is, at what time the Town was walled and is so remaining in good repair, having 6 Gates for entrance, and 15 Watch-towers for defence, extending in compass to 1500 paces: and whence the North-Pole is observed to be raised 52 deg. 27 min. in latitude, and is set from the first point of the West in longitude 17 deg. and 30 min. being yearly governed by a Mayor, chosen out of one and thirty Citizens, which are commonly called the Election, and he ever after is known for an Alderman, & clothed in scarlet, whereof four of the eldest are Justices of the Peace, graced with a Sword-bearer, a Recorder, a Town-clerk, & four Ser-geants with Maces.

The greatest glory that this City received, was in King Athelstan's daies; whereas Malmesbury doth report, he caused the Lords of Wales by way of tribute, to pay yearly (besides hawks and hounds) 20 pound of Gold, and 300 pound of Silver by weight: but how that was performed and continued, I find not.

This Counties climate is most healthful and temperate, and soil so fertile for Corn and Cattel, that no place in England yieldeth more or better conditoned: sweet Rivers running as veins in the body, do make the Corn-bearing grounds in some of her parts rightly to be termed the Gilden vale: and for Waters, Wooll, and Wheat, doth contend with Nilus, Colchos, and Aegypt: such are Lemster, and Irchenfeild, the banks of Wye, Luge, and Frome'.

¶ Much information is included, with over 30 references to streets and buildings. The numbered part of the key sensibly starts at '3' to avoid confusion with 'I' and 'Z'. In his description of the county Speed makes no mention of any cider production at that time, so the rather nondescript tree in the lower right-hand corner may or may not be significant.

HEREFORD

Black Friers

Wydmarsh Gate

Bisters Gate

Eygne Gate

S. Owyns Gate

William Hospital

S. Owyns

S. Gilles

Friers Gate

Bartesham prebend

Whit Friers

Wye flu.

A	Alhallowe
B	St. Peters
C	St Iohns
D	S. Ethelberts minst
E	St Nocholas
F	Kirryes Hospital
G	st Gilles Almeshous
H	St Ethelberts Almes
I	St Ethelberts Well
K	High Causye
L	Wyebrigd stret
M	Pipewell stretz
N	King Diche
O	Brode strete
P	Wroughtall
Q	Packers Lane
R	Bewall strete
S	Gilford stret
T	Northgate stret
V	Beyond the wall
W	Castle strete
X	Cabbage lane
Y	Hongery stretz
Z	The Castle
3	Bowsye lane
4	Wydmarsh strete
6	Iewry lane
7	S Thomas stret
8	Olde strete
9	Britons stret
0	Wye Bridge

A SCALE OF PASES

50   100   150   200

HERTFORD

'Many other Towns, both for Commerce, stately Buildings, and of ancient Record, this Shire affordeth whereof Hertford, though the Shire Town is not the richest; the passage thorow Ware hath left her ways so untrodden; to prevent which, in former times, that River at Ware was chained up, and the Bailiffs of Hertford had the custody of the Key: which howsoever they have lost, yet hath the Town gotten her Governour to be preferred from the name of a Bailiff, unto a Mayor, assisted with nine Burgesses, a Recorder, and two Sergeants their Attendants. Herein a Castle, for situation pleasant, for Trench, Walls, and River, sufficiently fenced, was lately seen; but marked to destiny, as the Town to decay, hath found the hand of Fortune to overmatch her strength, and to ruinate the Priorie St.Nicholas, and St.Maries Churches, besides a Cell of St.Albanes Monks, that therein were seated. The like fate falls unto Hemsted, and her fair Castle, wherein Richard King of the Romans left his life.

Yet Langley is graced both in the Birth of Prince Edmund the fifth son to King Edward the third, and the Burial of Richard the second, that unfortunate King, who in the Cell of Fryers Preachers was there first buried. but afterwards removed and enshrined at Westminster. And in another Langley, near and East from thence, was born that Pontifical Break-Spear, Bishop of Rome, known by the name of Hadrian the fourth, (and famous for his stirrup-holding by Frederick the Emperour) whose breath was at last stopped by a flie, that flew into his mouth.

Religious houses built and suppressed the chiefest for account in this Shire, were S.Albans, Royston, Ware, Sopwell, Langley, besides them at Hertford whom Beda calls Herudford: which Cities graduation is distant and removed from the Equator, 52 degrees, 5 minutes of latitude, and set from the first point of the West, according to Mercator, in the 20 degree 29 minutes of longitude'.

¶ The modest size of the county town did not prevent its inclusion by Speed, and in many other shires this was also the case. In his foreword he apologises for the absence of several of the most important towns of that time, but had decided that Shire towns should, whatever their size, be featured. Hertford is a clear example and Speed repeats his point in his text.

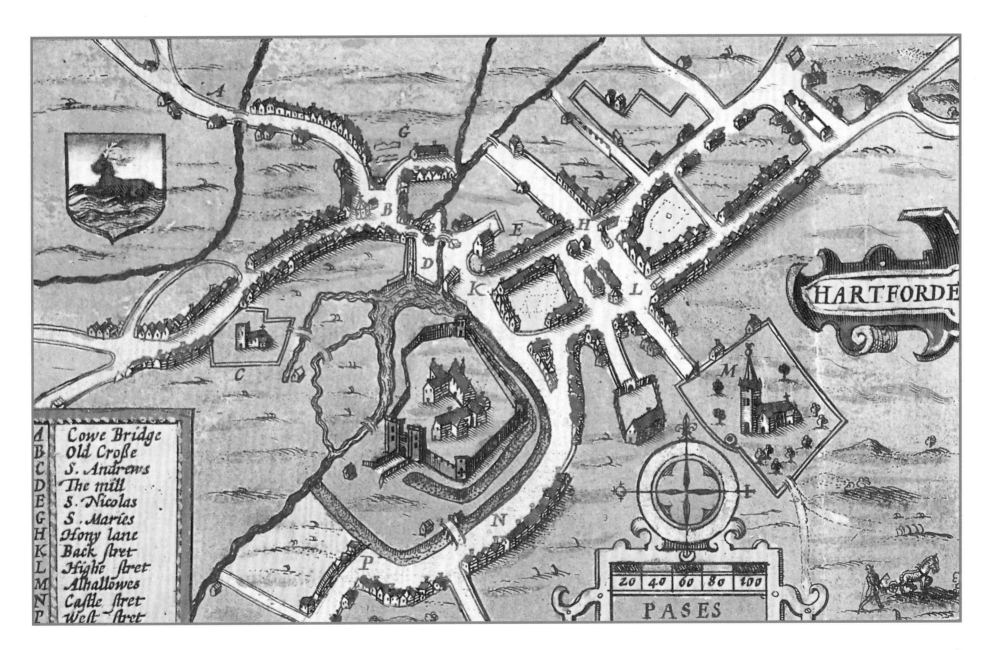

HARTFORDE

A Cowe Bridge
B Old Crosse
C S. Andrews
D The mill
E S. Nicolas
G S. Maries
H Hony lane
K Back stret
L Highe stret
M Alhallowes
N Castle stret
P West stret

PASES
20 40 60 80 100

HULL

'Places for trade and venting forth of her commodities are many, yet none of such convenience as Kingston upon Hull: which notwithstanding, cannot fetch her beginning from any great antiquity, being before time called Wike. King Edward the first built this Town making a Haven, and granting divers liberties to the Burgesses; so that it is risen to great state, both for stately buildings, and strong Block-houses for Ships, well furnished and store of Merchants, and is now become the most famous Town of that Country; whose greatest riches is ascribed to the gainful trade they have by Island-fish, dried and hardened, commonly called Stock-fish. This Town is governed by a Mayor (who hath the Sword of State carried before him) twelve Aldermen, that in their Assemblies go clad in Scarlet, one Sheriff, a Water-Bailiff, a Sword-bearer, a Chamberlain, a Recorder, a Town-clerk, and six Sergeants at Mace. Whose graduation according as the Mathematicks have observed, is for Longitude 20 degrees, and 30 scruples, and for Latitude 54 degrees and 28 scruples.

The Air is subtil and piercing, and not inclined naturally to contagious infections, which causeth the people to live long and healthfully, and are not so subject to Agues, fluxes, or other imperfections, as those Countries be, that are more troubled with mists or foggy vapours.

The soil is generally indifferently fruitful: for though some part be craggy, mountainous, and full of hills, yet some others exceeding good for the gifts of Nature in her delightsome varieties, as of Corn, Cattle, and Pasturage; with veins of Metal and Iron, besides an Allum earth of sundry colours, out of which some have lately begun to try very good Allum and Coperass. And for fish, the Hollanders and Zealanders do raise unto themselves great profit upon this Coast, having long since obtained licence, which they keep still by an ancient custom: for the Englishmen granting leave unto others, reserved the honour to themselves, which would be (no doubt) far the greater, if they made gain of their own labours.'

¶ The importance of Hull as a port and centre of commerce is apparent from this fine plan, and Speed makes full decorative use of the Humber and the River Hull for maritime embellishment. The windmills and figures in the countryside to the west are, as usual, not to the same scale as the plan; the horse for instance is larger than the ships in the River Hull. This would seem to be a perfectly reasonable approach as these vignettes are purely artistic.

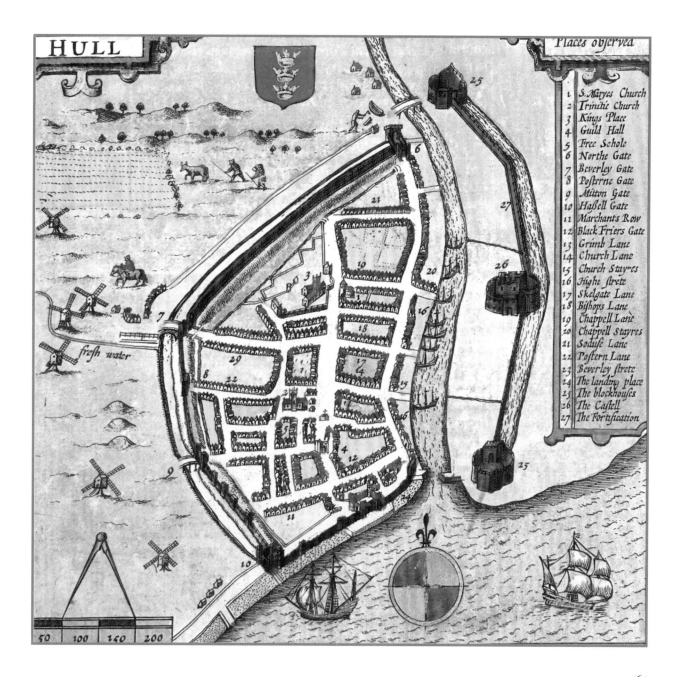

HULL

fresh water

50   100   150   200

63

HUNTINGDON

'The Shire-Town Huntingdon, Hundandun, or the Hunters-down, North, seated upon a rising bank, over the rich meadowed river Owse, interpreted by some Authors, the Down of Hunters, to which their now common Seal (a Hunter) seemeth to allude. Great and populous was this in the foregoing age, the following having here buried of fifteen all but three, besides the Mother Church S.Maries, in their own graves. At the reign of the Conqueror, it was ranged into four Ferlings or Wards, and in them 256. Burgenses or Husolds: It answered at all asseisments for 50 Hides, the fourth part of Hurstingston Hundred in which it standeth. The annual rent was then 30.l [£30] of which, as of three Minters there kept, the King had two parts, the Earl the third; the power of Coynage then and before, not being so privatively in the King but Borowes, Bishops and Earls enjoyed it; on the one side stamping the face and stile of their Soveraign, in acknowledgement of subordinacy in that part of absolute power, and on the reverse their own name, to warrant their integrity in that infinite trust.

The Castle supposed by some the work of the elder Edward, but seeming by the Book of Domesday, to be built by the Conqueror is now known but by the ruines: It was the seat of Walheof the great Saxon Earl, as of his succeeding heirs, until to end the question of right between Senilice and the King of Scots, Henry the second, laid it as you see; yet doth it remain the head of that honour on which in other Shires many Knights Fees, and sixteen in this attended. Here David Earl of this and Anguise, father of Isabel de Brus, founded the Hospital of St.John Baptist: and Lovetote here upon the Fee of Eustace the Viscount, built to the honour of the blessed Virgin, the Priory of Black Channons, valued at the suppression, 232.l.7.s.ob. [£232, seven shillings]. Here at the North end was a house of Fryers and without the Town at Hinching-brook, a Cloister of Nunnes, val.at 19.l 9.s.2d. founded by the first William in place of S.Pandonia, at Eltesley (by him suppressed) where neer the end of the last Henry the Family of the Cromwels began their Seat. To this Shire-town, and benefit of the neighbour Countries, this River was navigable until the power of Grey, a minion of the time, stopt that passage, and with it all redress either by Law or Parliament. By Charter of King John this Town hath a peculiar Coroner, profit by Toll and Custom, Recorder, Town-clerks, and two Bayliffs, (elected annually for government) as at Parliament, 2 Burgesses, for advice and assent: and is Lord of it self in Fee-Farm.'

HUNTINGTON

A	Bohne Holle
B	S. Iohns Church
C	The free Shole
D	St Georges
E	Alhallowes
F	The Shire Hall
G	Germans strete
H	St Benniets Church
I	The Jayle
K	S. Maryes Church
L	Cobblers lane
M	The bouling place
N	The water myll

THE SCALE OF PASES

50   100   150   200

¶ This small plan illustrates the arbitrary approach to spelling much in evidence throughout the atlas. The town's name is spelt Hunting*ton* both on the plan and on the county map, but in the text the 'don' ending is used, and elsewhere in the atlas the county is shown with various spellings including 'Huntingshire'. It might be thought that having the copperplates engraved in Amsterdam was partly to blame but Speed's descriptive text, which shows even greater variations, was printed on the reverse of the maps and the type was all set in London.

Ipswich

'The commodities of this Shire [Suffolk] are many and great, whereof the chiefest consist in Corn, Cattle, Cloth, Pasturage, Woods, Sea-fish and Fowle; and as Abbo floriecensis hath depainted, This County is of green and passing fresh hue, pleasantly replenished with Orchards, Gardens and Groves: thus he described it above six hundred years since, and now we find as he hath said; to which we may add their gain from the Pail, whose cheeses are traded not only throughout Enland, but into Germany, France, and Spain, and are highly commended by Pantaleon the Physitian, both for colour and tast.

And had Ipswich (the only eye of this Shire) been as fortunate in her Surname, as she is blessed with Commerce and buildings, she might worthily have borne the title of a City: neither ranked in the lowest row, whose trade, circuit, and seat, doth equal most places of the Land besides.

It seemeth this Town hath been walled about, both by a Rampire of earth, mounted along her North and West parts, and places of entrance where gates have stood; which no doubt, by the Danes were cast down, in the year of Christ Jesus 991. when they sacked with spoil all these Sea-coasts; and again in the year one thousand, laid the streets desolate, and the houses on heaps; yet afterwards recovering both breath and beauty, her buildings from Stoke-church in the South to S.Margarets in the North, now contain 1900 paces, and from S.Helens in the East, to S.Matthews Church in the West, are no less then 2120. full of streets plentyously inhabited, wherein are twelve Parish-churches seated, besides them suppressed such were Christ Church, S.Georges, S.James, the White, the Black and Gray-Friers. The Site of this Town is removed from the Equator unto the degree 52.25 minutes; and by Mercators observation, from the first West points 22.degrees, 9.minutes: and is yeerly governed by two Bailiffs and ten Port-men, all wearing Scarlet, with twenty four of their Common-counsel in purple: a Recorder, a Town-Clerk, five Sergeants, whereof one is for the Admiralty, a Beadle, and Common-Crier, all in blew, with the Towns Arms on their Sleeves.'

¶ This is a particularly fine town plan with 30 references in the key, ships on the river and a very fanciful vignette of the sun shining on a hillier landscape than exists in the Suffolk countryside surrounding Ipswich.

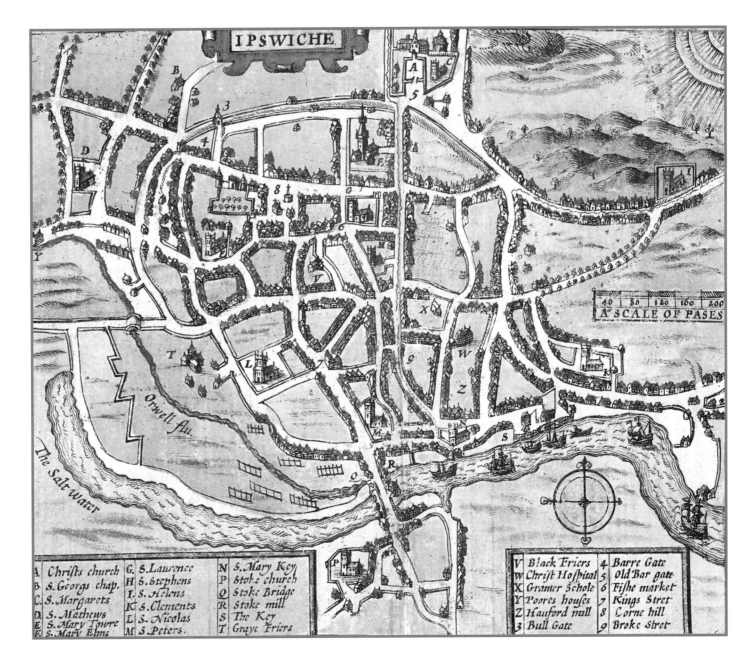

IPSWICHE

Orwell flu.

The Salt Water

A SCALE OF PASES
40 | 80 | 120 | 160 | 200

A	Christs church	G.	S. Laurence	N	S. Mary Key	V	Black Friers	4	Barre Gate
B	S. Georgs chap.	H	S. Stephens	O	Stoke church	W	Christ Hospital	5	Old Bar gate
C	S. Margarets	I	S. Helens	P	Stoke Bridge	X	Gramer Schole	6	Fishe market
D	S. Mathews	K	S. Clements	Q	Stoke mill	Y	Poores houses	7	Kings Stret
E	S. Mary Towre	L	S. Nicolas	R	The Key	Z	Hauford mill	8	Corne hill
F	S. Mary Elms	M	S. Peters.	T	Graye Friers	3	Bull Gate	9	Broke Stret

67

KENDAL

'The chiefest place [in Westmorland] is Kandale or Kendale, called also Kirkeby Kendale, standing on the bank of the River Can. This Town is of great trade and resort, and for the diligent and industrious practise of making cloth so excels the rest, that in regard thereof it carrieth a super-eminent name above them, and hath great vent and traffick for her woollen Cloaths through all the parts of England. It challengeth not much glory for Antiquity, only this it accounteth a great credit, that it hath dignified three Earls with the title thereof, as John Duke of Bedford, whom Henry the fifth (being his Brother) advanced to that honour, John Duke of Sommerset, and John de Foiz, whom King Henry the sixth preferred to that dignity for his honourable and trusty services done in the French Wars. It is a place of very civil and orderly government, the which is mannaged by an Alderman, chosen every year out of his twelve Brethren, who are all distinguished and notified from the rest by the wearing of purple garments. The Alderman and his Senior Brother are always Justices of Peace and Quorum. There are in it a Town-Clerk, a Recorder, two Sergeants at Mace, and two Chamberlains. By Mathematical observation the site of this Town is in the degree of Longitude 17.30.scruples, from the first West-point, and the Pole elevated in Latitude to the degree 55.and 15 minutes.

The Soil for the most part of it, is but barren, and can hardly be brought to any fruitfulness by the industry and painful labour of the Husbandman being so full of infertile places, which the Northern Englishmen call Moors: yet the more Southerly part is not reported to be so sterile, but more fruitful in the Vallies, though contained in a narrow room, between the River Lone, and Winander-mear, and it is all termed by one name. The Barony of Kendale or Candale, that is the dale by Can, taking the name of the River Can that runs through it.'

¶ This is one of very few plans to be narrower than its height, making enlargement here less easy. Though not based on Speed's own survey, his engraver has typically added a few figures to provide light relief. The spelling of the town's name on this plan (Kendale) differs from that on the county map of Westmorland (Kendall), again illustrating the lack of precision or consistency through-out the atlas.

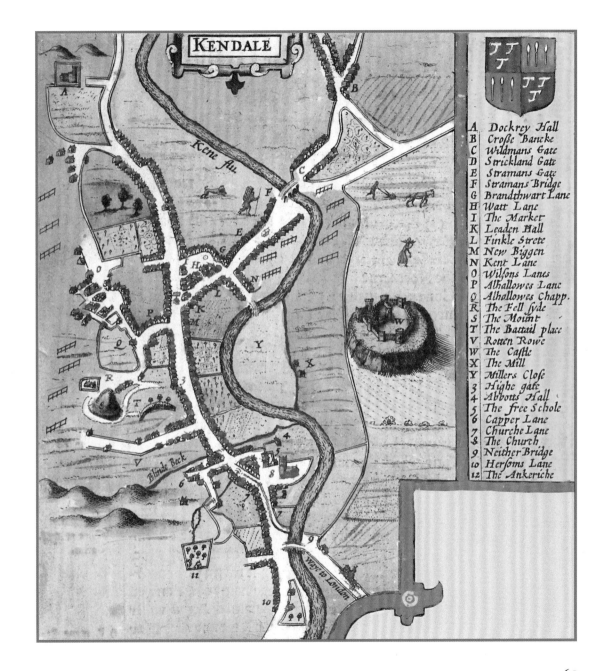

KENDALE

Kent flu.

Blind Beck

Way to Lonsum

A	Dockrey Hall
B	Croße Bancke
C	Wildmans Gate
D	Strickland Gate
E	Stramans Gate
F	Stramans Bridge
G	Brandthwart Lane
H	Watt Lane
I	The Market
K	Leaden Hall
L	Finkle Strete
M	New Biggen
N	Kent Lane
O	Wilsons Lanes
P	Alhallowes Lane
Q	Alhallowes Chapp.
R	The Fell syde
S	The Mount
T	The Battail place
V	Rotten Rowe
W	The Castle
X	The Mill
Y	Millers Close
3	Highe gate
4	Abbotts Hall
5	The free Schole
6	Capper Lane
7	Churche Lane
8	The Church
9	Neither Bridge
10	Hersoms Lane
12	The Ankeriche

LANCASTER

'The Shire-town is Lancaster, more pleasant in situation, than rich of Inhabitants, built on the South of the River Lon, and is the same Longovicum, where (as we find in the Notice Provinces) a company of the Longonicarins under the Lieutenant General of Britain lay. The beauty of this Town is in the Church, Castle, and Bridge: her streets many, and stretched far in length. Unto this Town King Edward the third granted a Major and two Bailiffs, which to this day are elected out of twelve Brethren assisted by twenty four Burgesses, by whom it is yearly governed, with the supply of two Chamberlains, a Recorder, Town-Clerk, and two Sergeants at Mace. The elevation of whose pole is in the degree of Latitude 54 and 58 scruples, and her longitude removed from the first West point unto the degree 17 and 40 scruples.

The Air subtile and piercing, not troubled with gross vapours or foggie mists, by reason whereof the people of that Country live long and healthfully, and are not subject to strange and unknown diseases. The soil for the generality is not very fruitful, yet it produceth such numbers of Cattle, of such large proportion, and such goodly heads, and horns, as the Kingdom of Spain doth scarce the like.

It is a Country replenished with all necessaries for the use of man, yielding without any great labour the commodity of Corn, flax, Grass, Coals, and such like. The Sea also adding her blessing to the Land, that the people of that Province want nothing that serves either for the sustenance of nature, or the satiety of Appetite. They are plentifully furnished with all sorts of fish, flesh, and Fowls. Their principal fuel is Coal and Turf, which they have in great abundance, the Gentlemen reserving their woods very carefully, as a beauty and principal ornament to their Mannors and Houses. And though it be far from London (the Capital City of this Kingdom) yet doth it every year furnish her and many other parts of the Land besides, with many thousands of Cattle (bred in this Country) giving thereby and otherwise a firm testimony to the world, of the blessed abundance that it hath pleased God to enrich this noble Dukedom withall.'

§ This plan is one of the plainest, although it appears on one of the most dramatic of the maps featuring royal portraits of the houses of Lancaster and York. The letters on the coat of arms indicate colours, using the heraldic French terms, to guide both amateurs and professionals when applying watercolours (see p.118).

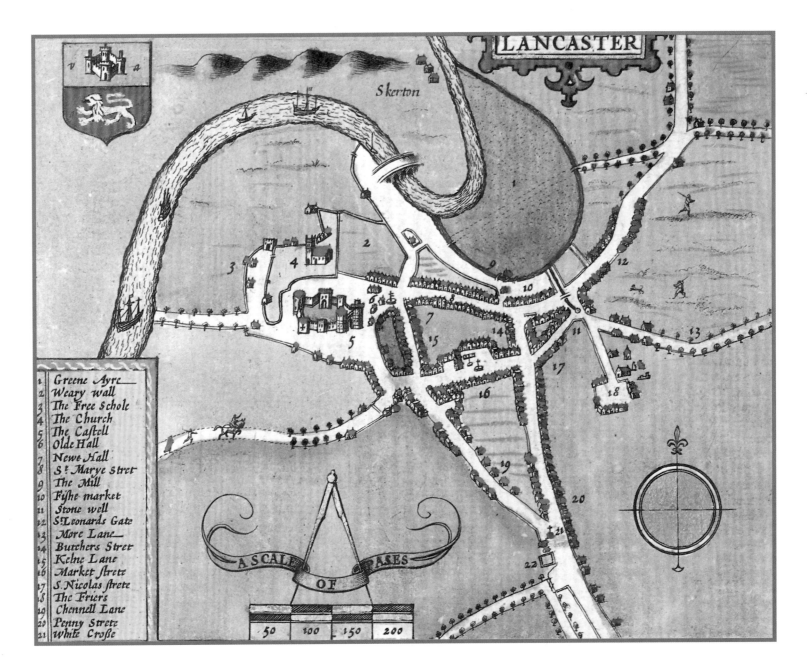

LANCASTER

Skerton

1. Greene Ayre
2. Weary wall
3. The Free Schole
4. The Church
5. The Castell
6. Olde Hall
7. Newe Hall
8. St. Marye stret
9. The Mill
10. Fishe market
11. Stone well
12. St. Leonards Gate
13. More Lane
14. Butchers Stret
15. Kelne Lane
16. Market strete
17. S. Nicolas strete
18. The Friers
19. Chennell Lane
20. Penny Strete
21. White Croße

A SCALE OF PASES

50   100   150   200

71

LEICESTER

'From this Town the Shire hath the name, though the name of herself is diversly written, as Legecestria, Leogora, Legeo-cester: by Ninius, Caer-Lerion; by Matthew of Westminster (if we do not mistake him) Wiral; and now lastly Leices-ter: ancient enough if King Leir was her builder, 844 years before the birth of our Saviour, wherein he placed a flamine to serve in the Tem-ple of Janus, by himself there erected, and where he was buried, if Geffrey ap Arthur say true: but now certain it is, that Ethelred the Mercian Monarch, made it an Episcopal See, in the year of Christ Jesus 680, wherein Sexwulph of his elec-tion became the first Bishop: which shortly after was thence translated, and therewith the beauty of the Town began to decay; upon whose desolations that erectifying Lady Edelfled cast her eyes of compassion, and both reedified the build-ings, and compassed it about with a strong wall, where in short time the Cities trade so increased, that Matthew Paris in his lesser Story reporteth as

followeth, 'Lege-cester (saith he) is a right wealthy City, and notably defended; and had the wall a sure foundation, were inferior to no City whatsoever'. But this pride of prosperity lasted not long under the Normans, for it was sore oppressed with a world of calamities, when Robert Bossu the crouch-back Earl of that Prov-ince, rebelled against his Soveraign Lord King Henry the Second: whereof hear the same Author Paris speak: 'Through the obstinate stubbornness of Earl Robert (saith he) the noble City Leicester was besieged and thrown down by King Henry, and the wall that seemed indissoluble was utterly raced, even to the ground.' The pieces of whose fragments so fallen down, remained in his days like to hard Rocks, through the strength of the Morter cementing whole lumps together: and at the Kings command the City was set on fire and burnt, the Castle raced, and an heavy imposition laid upon the Citizens, who with great sums of money bought their own banishments: but were

so used in their departure that for extreme fear many of them took Sanctuary both at S.Edmunds and S.Albans. In repentance of these mischiefs, the Author thereof Earl Robert, built the Monas-tery of S Mary de Pratis wherein himself became a Canon Regular, and for fifteen years continuance in sad laments served God in continual Prayers. With the like devotion Henry the first Duke of Lancaster built an Hospital for an hundred and ten poor people, with a Collegiate Church, a Dean, twelve Canons Prebendaries, as many Vicars sufficiently provided for with revenues; wherein himself lieth buried: and it was the greatest ornament of that City, until the hand of King Henry the Eighth lay over-heavy upon all the like foundations, and laid their aspired tops at his own feet.' ⚜

¶ This plan, not based on a survey by Speed, has no com-pass or other orientation, but seems to be more or less conventional with north being at the top, although a little tilted. The panel 'performed by John Speede' &c refers to the county map and not the town plan.

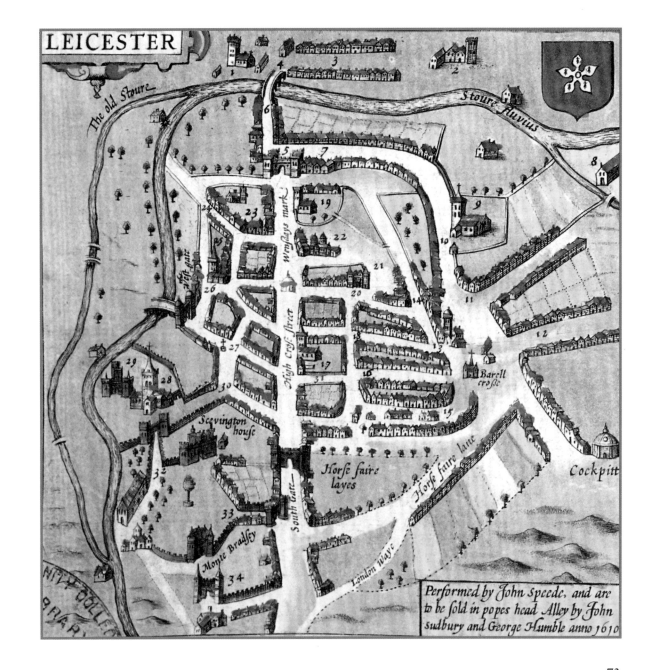

Chief places of yᵉ Citie by figures noted

1	S. Leonards	18	S Martins street
2	Leicester Abbey	19	Alhallowes
3	Abbey gate	20	High street
4	Sundays bridge	21	Huntington place
5	North gate	22	Woole Hall
6	North gate street	23	Graye fryers
7	Sinuis gate	24	Graye fryers gate
8	The Spittle	25	S Nicholas
9	S. Margrets	26	S Nicholas shambles
10	Churche gate	27	Redd crosse street
11	Belgrave gate	28	S Maryes
12	Humberston gate	29	The Castell
13	East Gate	30	Castell street
14	Swines market	31	Black fryers lane
15	Satterdayes market	32	Ould Hospitall
16	Cankwell Lane	33	The newe warke
17	S. Martines	34	The Grange

LICHFIELD

'But Lichfeild, more large, and of far greater fame, is much more ancient, [than Stafford]. Known unto Beda by the name of Licidfeild, which Rosse doth interpret to be The field of dead bodies, for the number of Saints under the rage of Dioclesian there slain: upon which cause the City beareth for her Arms an Escocheon of Landskip, with divers Martyrs in divers manner massacred. Here Oswin King of Northumberland overcoming the Pagan-Mercians, built a Church, and made it the See of Duina the Bishop; whose successors grown rich, with golden reasons so overcame King Offa, and he Adrian the Pope, that an Archiepiscopal Pale was granted Bishop Eadulph, to the great disgrace of Lambert Arch-bishop of Canterbury. In this Church were interred the bodies of Wulfhere and Celred, both of them Kings of the Mercians. But when the minds of men were set altogether upon gorgeous building, this old foundation was new reared by Roger Clinton, Bishop of this See, and dedicated to the Virgin Mary and Saint Chad, and the Close inwalled by Bishop Langton. The Government of this City is by two Bayliffs, and one Sheriff, yearly chosen out of 24 Burgesses, a Recorder, a Town-Clerk, and two Sergeants their Attendants.

Houses of Religion erected in this Shire were at Lichfeild, Stafford de la Cross, Cruxden, Trentham, Burton, Tamworth and Wolverhampton. These Votaries abusing their Founders true pieties, and heaping up riches with disdain of the Laity, laid themselves open as marks to be shot at; whom the hand of the skilful soon hit, and quite pierced, under the aim of King Henry the Eighth, who with such revenues in most places relieved the poor and the orphan with schools and maintenance for the training up of youth: a work (no doubt) more acceptable to God, and of more charitable use to the Land.'

❡ Probably the most striking feature of this plan is the illustration of the arms of the city, which Speed describes as a landscape showing martyrs being slain. The domination of the cathedral is clear, but the figures in the fields are of more modest size than in most other cases, and are those swans in the lakes?

Places in the Citie Lichfield by figures observed

1	Stowe Church	18	Wade Street
2	Stowe Mill	19	Towne Hall
3	Stowe Street	20	Frogge lane
4	Ioyles lane	21	St Iohns street
5	St. Michaels chur.	22	St Iohns Hospitall
6	Rotten Rowe	23	The Friery
7	Tamworth stret	24	The Conduit
8	The Chappell	25	The Freeschole
9	The Conduit	26	Grey Marger lane
10	Dams street	27	Greenehill street
11	St Chads minst.	28	Bakers lane
12	Iayes lane	29	Friers lane
13	Bacon stret	30	High Crosse
14	The Almeshouse	31	Stowe Crosse
15	Samford stret	32	Damm Mill
16	Sadlers street	33	Stowe Mere
17	Bore street	34	Damm Mere

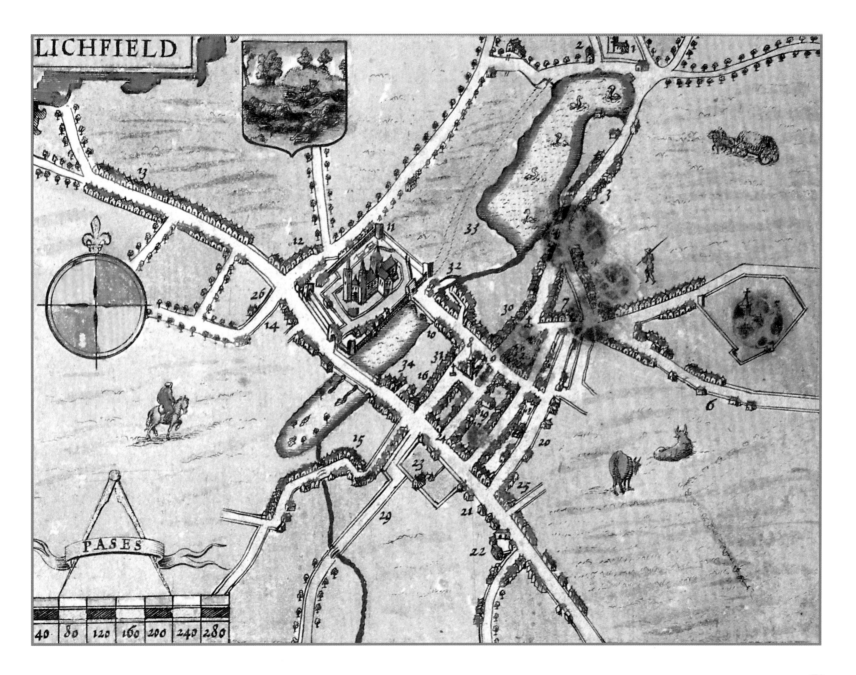

LICHFIELD

PASES

| 40 | 80 | 120 | 160 | 200 | 240 | 280 |

LINCOLN

'Trade and Commerce for provision of life is vented thorow thirty one Market-towns in this Shire, whereof Lincolne the Counties name is chief, by Ptolomy and Antonie called Lindum, by Beda Linde-collina, by the Saxons Lyndo-collyne, and the Normans, Nichol. Very ancient it is, and hath been more magnifical, as by her many over-turned ruines doth appear, and far more popu-lous, as by Domesdays book is seen, where it is recorded that this City contained a thousand and seven Mansions, and nine hundred Burgesses, with twelve Lage-men, having Sac and Soc. And in the Normans time, satith [saith] Malmesbury, it was one of the best peopled Cities of England, being a place for traffick of Merchandize for all comers by Land or Sea. Herein King Ewd.3 the ordained his Staple for the Mart of Woolls, Leathe, and Lead, no less than fifty Parish-Churches did beautifie the same: but now containeth only fifteen besides the Cathedral. Some ruines yet remains both of Frieries and Nunneries, who lie now buried in their own ashes, and the City conquered not by War, but by time and very age; and yet hath she not escaped the calamity of Sword, as in the time of the Saxons; whence Arthur enforcing their Host: the like also did Edmund to the destroying Danes; and by the Normans it suffered some damage, where King Stephen was vanquished and taken prisoner; and again by the third Henry that assaulted and wan from his rebellious Barons. By fire likewise it was sore defaced, wherein not only the buildings were consumed, but withal many men and women in the violence thereof perished: as also by an Earthquake her foundation was much weakened and shaken, wherein the fair Cathedral Church, dedicated to the Virgin of Virgins, was rent to pieces.

The Government of this City is committed yearly to a Mayor, two Sheriffs, twelve Aldermen in Scarlet, a Sword, a Hat of Estate, a Recorder, Sword-bearer, and four Sergeants with Maces: whose situation on a steep hill standeth, for longitude in the degree 20.10 scruples, the Pole elevated for Latitude from the degree 53. and 50 scruples.'

¶ This is the only plan not illustrated in its entirety in this book. The original by Speed had an extended por-tion to the south-east (in the shape of a shoe) and a small part on the eastern extremity of this has been cropped here to allow sufficient enlargement of the city plan. Just to add a little further confusion, the plan is orientated with north to the left-hand side.

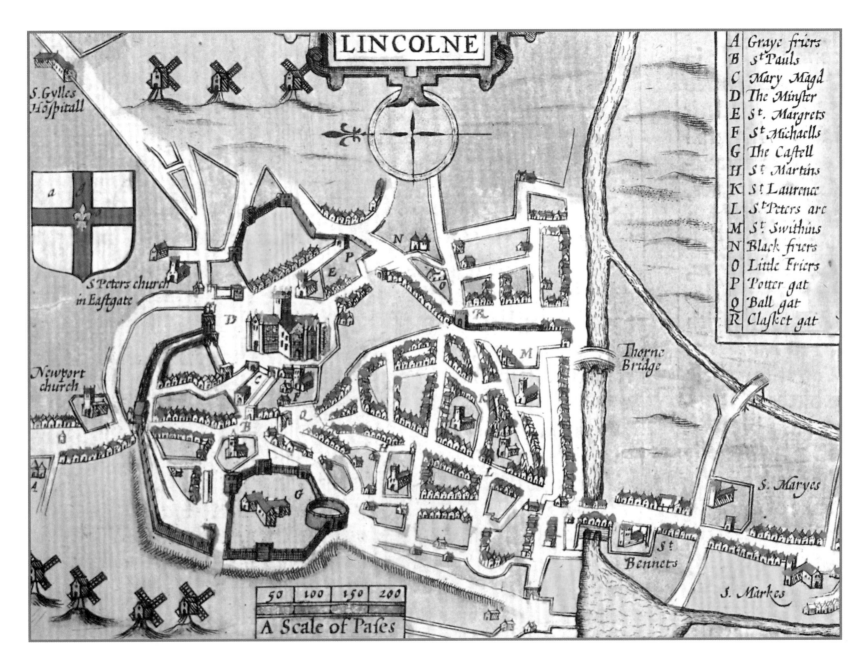

LINCOLNE

A Graye friers
B St Pauls
C Mary Magd
D The Minster
E St. Margrets
F St. Michaells
G The Castell
H St. Martins
K St Laurence
L St Peters arc
M St Swithins
N Black friers
O Little Friers
P Potter gat
Q Ball gat
R Clasket gat

S. Gylles Hospitall

S Peters church in Eastgate

Newport church

Thorne Bridge

S. Maryes

St Bennets

S. Markes

50 100 150 200

A Scale of Pases

London

'Which City is more ancient than any true record beareth, fabuled from Brute, Troynovant, from Lud Ludstone: But by more credible Writers, Tacitus, Ptolomy, and Antonine, Londinium, by Aminianus Mercellinus for her successive prosperity, Augusta, the greatest title that can be given to any: by Britains, Londain, by the Saxons Londoncearden, by Strangers Londra, and by us London. This City doth shew as the Cedars among other trees, being the seat of the British Kings, the Chamber of the English, the Model of the Land, and the Mart of the World: for thither are brought the Silk of Asia, the spices from Africa, the Balms from Grecia, and the Riches of both the Indies East and West: no City standing so long in fame, nor any for divine and politick government may with her be compared. Her Walls were first set by great Constantine the first Christian Emperor, at the suit of his Mother, Queen Helen, reared with rough Stone and British Brick three English miles in compass; thorow which are now made seven most fair Gates, besides three other passages for entrance. Along the Thamesis this Wall at first ranged and with two Gates opened, the one Doure-gate, now Dowgate and the other Billinsgate, a receptacle for Ships. In the midst of this Wall was set a mile-mark (as the like was in Rome) from whence were measured their stations, for carriage or otherwise; the same as yet standeth, and hath been long known by the name of London-stone. Upon the East of this City, the Church of St.Peters is thought to be the Cathedral of Restitutus, the Christian Bishops See, who lived in the Reign of Great Constantine; but since St.Pauls in the West part, from the Temple of Diana assumed that Dignity, whose Greatness doth exceed any other at this day, and spires so high, that twice it hath been consumed by lightening from Heaven. Besides this Cathedral, God is honoured in one hundred twenty one Churches more in this City: that is, ninety six within the Walls: sixteen without, but within the Liberties; and nine more in her Suburbs; and in fitz-Stephens time, thirteen Convents of religious Orders. It is divided into twenty six Wards, governed by so many grave Aldermen, a Lord Mayor and two Sheriffs, the yearly choice whereof was granted them by Patent from K.John; in whose time also a Bridge of Stone was made over Thames upon 19 arches, for length, bredth, beauty and building, the like again not found in the world.' ❧

[*Continued in the description of Westminster*]

❡ The plan of the capital city is particularly fine, though not by Speed. However the presence of a 'Scale of Paces' is confusing. If, as seems certain, Speed only included the scale on plans that resulted from his own surveys, then London should not have one. The first edition of his map of Middlesex did omit the scale-bar title on the London plan, but it had been added by the second edition (1614). In the text engraved on the face of the map he states 'the trew plott whereof I purposely reserve to a further leasure and a larger scale'. I cannot trace any plan of London by Speed but he obviously intended to produce one and no doubt did his own survey of the city in which he lived in preparation for this. It seems probable that having established the distances within the city he then confirmed the scale-bar on his already published map.

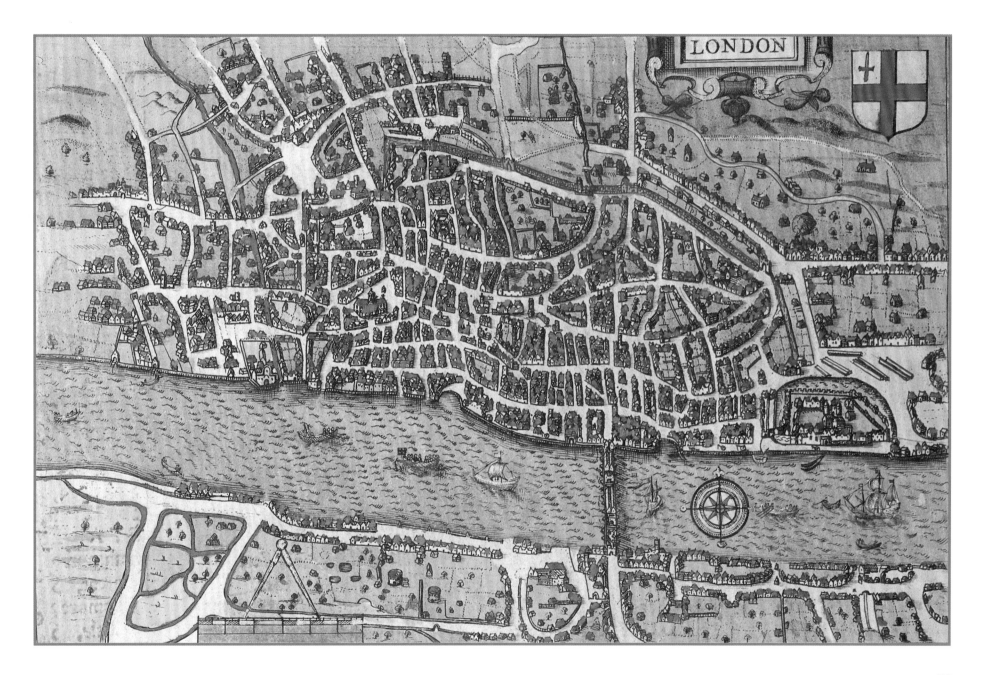

79

NEWCASTLE

'The chiefest commodity that enricheth this County are those stones Linthancraces, which we call Sea-coals, whereof there is such plenty and abundance digged up, as they do not only return a great gain to the Inhabitants, but procure also much pleasure and profit to others. No place in this Province vents forth so many of these Sea-coals into other regions as Newcastle doth, being the very eye of all the Towns in this County: for it doth not only minister relief (by such provision) to all other parts of England, but doth also furnish the wants of forein Countries with her plenty. By means of this and the intercourse of Traffick which it hath, the place is grown exceeding rich and populous. Before the Conquest it was called Monkchester: having been (as it seemed) in the possession of Monks: and Chester being added which signifies a bulwark or place of defence, shows that in ancient time it had been a place of fortification.

After the Conquest it got the name of Newcastle, by the new Castle which Robert the Son of William the Conqueror, built there, out of the ground. What it was called in old time is not known, yet some are of opinion, that it may be thought to have been Gatrosentum, for that Gateshead, the suburb (as it were) of the same, expresseth in the own proper signification that British name, Gatrosentum. It is now most ennobled both by the Haven (which Tyne maketh) of that notable depth, that it beareth very tall Ships, and is able to defend them against storms and tempests. As also by the favours and honours wherewith it hath been dignified by Princes: for Richard the second granted that a Sword should be carried before the Mayor, and Henry the sixth made it a County consisting of a Corporation within it self. It is adorned with four Churches, and fortified with strong walls that have eight gates. It is distant from the first West line 21 degrees and 30 minutes, and from the Equinoctial line towards the North-pole 34 degrees and 57 minutes.' ❧

¶ This plan includes a scale of paces and an attribution to William Mathew. As Speed only gave a scale for plans based on his own surveys, it is clear that, as with the plan of Berwick, he used an existing drawing as the basis. He then completed his work using the information and measurements from his own visit to the city. The use of Newe-Castle in the title is at variance with the spelling used in the text, and on the body of the map of Northumberland, and shows again the contemporary approach to orthography.

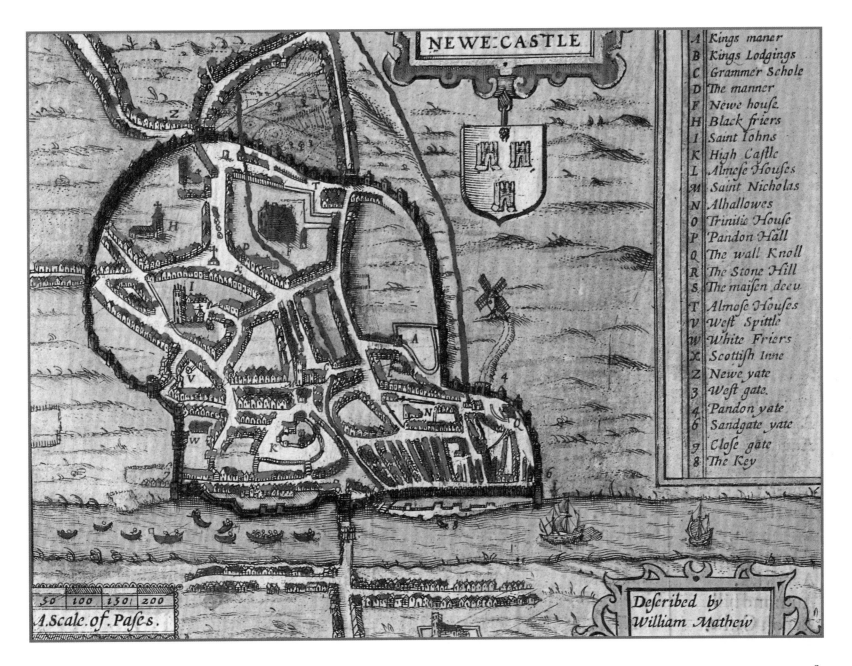

NEWE CASTLE

A	Kings maner
B	Kings Lodgings
C	Grammer Schole
D	The manner
F	Newe house
H	Black friers
I	Saint Iohns
K	High Castle
L	Almese Houses
M	Saint Nicholas
N	Alhallowes
O	Trinitie House
P	Pandon Hall
Q	The wall Knoll
R	The Stone Hill
S	The maisen deeu
T	Almose Houses
V	West Spittle
W	White Friers
X	Scottish Inne
Z	Newe yate
3	West gate
4	Pandon yate
6	Sandgate yate
9	Close gate
8	The Key

50 100 130 200

A Scale of Pases.

Described by
William Matheiw

NEWPORT (Isle of Wight)

'The principal Market-town in the Isle is Newport, called in times past Medena, and Novus Burgus de Meden; that is, the new Burgh of Meden, whereof the whole country [county] is divided into East-Meden, and West-Meden. A Town well seated, and much frequented; unto whose burgesses his Majesty hath lately granted the choice of a Mayor, who with his Brethren doth govern accordingly. It is populous with inhabitants, having an entrance into the Isle from the Haven, and a passage for Vessels of small burden unto the Key. Not far from it is the Castle Caresbrook, whose Founder is said to have been Whitgar the Saxon, and from him called White-Garesburgh; but now made shorter for easier pronunciation; the graduation whereof for latitude is in the degree 50.36 minutes: and her longitude in 19.4 minutes, where formerly hath stood a Priory, and at Quarre a Nunnery; a necessary neighbour to those Penitentiaries. And yet in their merry mood the inhabitants of this Island do boast, that they were happier than their neighbour Countries, for that they never had Monk that ever wore hood, Lawyers that cavilled, nor Foxes that were crafty.

It is reported, that in the year of mans salvation, 1167 and twenty three of King Henry the second, that in this Island it rained a shower of blood, which continued for the space of two hour together, to the great wonder and amazement of the people that beheld it with fear.

This Isle of Wight is fortified both by Art and Nature: for besides the strength of artificial Forts and Block-houses(wherewith it is well furnished) it wants not the assistance of natural fences, as being enriched with a continual ridge and range of craggy cliffs, and rocks, and banks, very dangerous for Sailers, as the Needles, so called by reason of their sharpness, the Shingles, Mixon, Brambles &c.'

¶ This plan corresponds generally with modern Newport, and Speed's survey identifies the main streets, nearly all of which still exist. Although his description of the Isle of Wight refers to Carisbrooke Castle, his plan of Newport does not extend quite far enough to include it, and its importance today owes more to Charles I's imprisonment (37 years after Speed's publication) than to its earlier history.

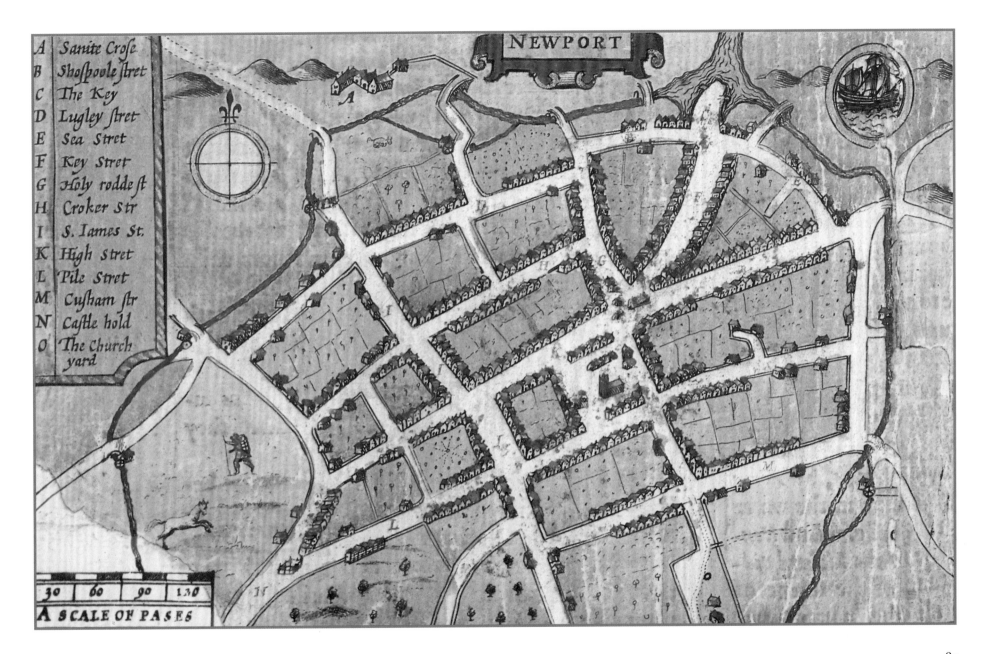

NEWPORT

A | Sante Crose
B | Shosspoole stret
C | The Key
D | Lugley stret
E | Sea Stret
F | Key Stret
G | Holy rodde st
H | Croker Str
I | S. Iames St.
K | High stret
L | Pile Stret
M | Cusham str
N | Castle hold
O | The Church yard

30 60 90 120
A SCALE OF PASES

NORTHAMPTON

'The chief Town in this Shire is Northampton, whereof the County taketh name, which for circuit, beauty and building, may be ranked with the most of the Cities of our Land. It is seated at the meeting and confluence of two rivers, the greater whereof beareth to name Nen. This Town hath been built all of stone, as by many foundations remaining to this day is seen, and is walled about both strong and high, excepting the West, which is defended by a River parted into many streams. In the depredations of the Danes, Sven their King set this Town on fire, and afterwards it was sorely assaulted by the disobedient Barons of King John, who named themselves The Army of God: but the loyalty of this Town stood nothing so sure unto King Henry his Son, whence the Barons with displayed Banners sounded the Battel against their Soveraign. And yet after this a woful field of Englands civil division was fought, whence Richard Nevil the stout Earl of Warwick led away prisoner that unfortunate man King Henry the Sixth. Upon the West part of this Town standeth a large Castle mounted upon an Hill, whose aged countenance well showeth the beauty she hath born, and whose gaping chinks do daily threaten the downfal of her walls. To this upon the South the towns wall adjoyneth and in a round circuit meeteth the River in the North, extending in compass two thousand one hundred and twenty paces: whose site so pleased the Students of Cambridge, that hither they removed themselves upon the Kings warrant, in mind to have made it an University: from whence the North-pole is elevated 52 degrees 36 scruples for latitude, and in longitude is removed from the West 19 degrees and 40 scruples, being yearly governed by a Mayor, two Bailiffs, twelve Magistrates, a Recorder, Town-clerk, a Common-Counsel of forty eight Burgesses, with five Sergeants to execute business.

The air is good, temperate, and healthful; the soil is champion, rich and fruitful, and so plenteously peopled, that from some Ascents thirty Parish-Churches and many more Windmills at one view may be seen: notwithstanding the simple and gentle sheep, of all creatures the most harmless, are now become so ravenous that they begin to devour men, wast fields, and depopulate houses, if not whole Townships, as one merrily hath written.'

¶ Considering the size and importance of the town in the 17th century, more references in the key might have been expected. Certainly in his text, Speed shows a high regard for the town, and then, as now, there was evidence of justifiable aspiration to city status.

NORTHAMPTON

A	St Andrews mill	G	Marhold	N	The Hermitage	T	The Towre
B	S Andrews Abbey	H	Graye Friers	O	S. Iames end	V	Darngate
C	North Gate	I	The Drapery	P	Bridge stret	W	St Thomas well
D	St Sepulchres	K	S Kathrens	Q	St Iohns	X	St Gylles
E	Sheepe market	L	The Checker	R	Alhallowes	Y	Free Schole
F	S Edmonds end	M	The Castell	S	St Peters	Z	The Mill

Scale of Pases

40 80 120 160 200 040

85

Norwich

'The Towns here [Norfolk] are commonly well built and populous; three of them being of that worth and quality, as no one Shire of England hath the like, Norwich, Lenn, and Yarmouth: to which, for ancient reputation, (as having been a seat of the Kings of East-Angles) I may add Thetford, known to Antoninus, and elder ages, by the name of Sitomagus, when the other three were yet in their infancy, and of no esteem: for I accept not the relations of the Antiquity and state of Norwich in the time of the Britains and Saxons, though Alexander Nevil hath well graced them. Her very name abridgeth her Antiquity, as having no other in Histories but Norwich, which is meer Saxon or Danish, and signifieth the North Town, Castle, or winding of a River. It seemeth to have risen out of the decay of her neighbour Venta, now called Castor; and as the Master Camden noteth, not to have been of mark before the entry of the Danes, who in the year 1004, under Sweno, their Captain, first sackt, and then burnt it, even in her infancy. Yet in the days of Edward the Confessor it recovered to 1320 Burgesses. But maintaining the cause of Earl Radulph aforesaid against the Conquerer they were by famine and sword wasted to 560. At which time the Earl escaping by Ship his Wife upon composition yielded the Castle, and followed. In William Rufus time it was grown famous for Merchandize and concourse of people; so that Herbert then translating the Bishopric from Thetford thither, made each of them an ornament to other. In variety of times it felt much variety of fortune: by fire in Anno 1508. By extreme plagues, whereof one in Anno 1348 was so outragious as 57104 are reported to have died thereof between the Calends of January and July. By misery of war, as sacked and spoyled by the Earl of flanders, and Hugh Bigad, Ann.1174. In yielding to Lewis the French against their natural Lord King John, ann.1216. By the disinherited Barons, an.1266. By tumult and insurrection between the Citizens and Church-men: once about the year 1265; which if Henry the third had not come in person to appease, the City was in hazard to be ruined. The second time in ann.1446, for which the Major [mayor] was deposed, and their Liberties for a while seized. In Edward the sixth time, by Ketts rebellion, whose fury chiefly raged against this City. Since this it hath flourished with the blessings of Peace, Plenty, Wealth, and Honour: so that Alexander Nevil doubteth not to prefer it above all the Cities of England, except London. It is situate upon the River Hierus, in a pleasant valley, but on rising ground, having on the East the Hills and Heath called Mussold, for Mosswould, as I take it. In the 17th year of King Stephen it was new founded, and made a Corporation. In Edward the firsts time closed with a fair wall, saving on a part that the River defended. first governed by four Bayliffs, then by Henry the fourth, ann.1403 erected into a Mayoralty and County. the limits whereof now extend to Eaton-bridge. At this present it hath about thirty Parishes, but in ancient time had many more.'

¶ This plan is one of the minority that were not Speed's own work, being copied from William Smith's of 1588, which in turn was based on William Cuningham's of 1559. The engraving is clearly not by Hondius, and is from one of the few map plates engraved for the atlas by Renold Elstrack, whose name appears on the map of Norfolk from the 1623 edition.

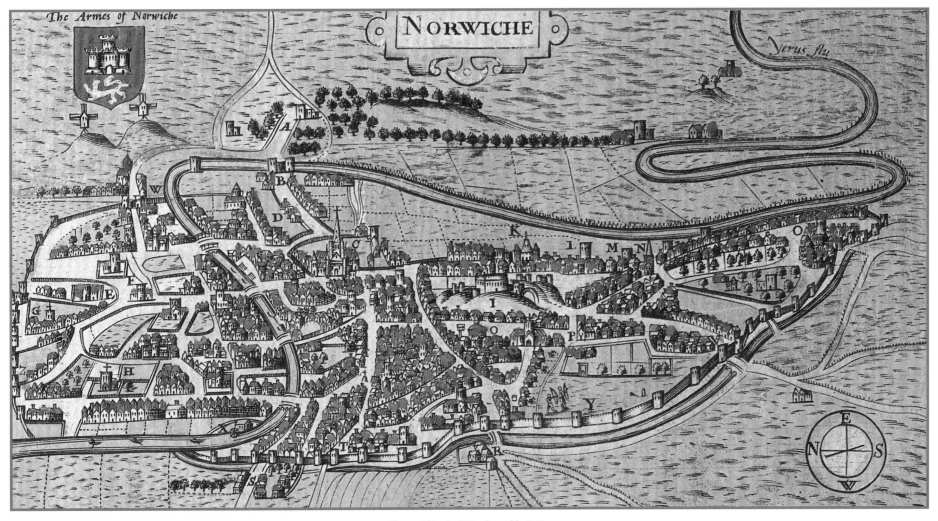

Places within the Citie observed by Letters

A S. Leonards	E S. Botholds	I The Castle	N S. Michaels	R S. Gyles gate	W Pockethorpe gate
B Bishopps gate	F S. Clements	K S. Peters Permantigate	O S. Johns at the gate	S Hell gate	X The New Milles
C The Cathedrall Churche	G S. Augustins	L S. Martins on the hill	P S. Stephens	T S. Benets gates	Y Chapell in the feilde
D S. Martins at ye Pallis gate	H S. Martins at the Oke	M S. Johns on the hill	Q The Market place	V S. Stephens gates	Z S. Martins gate

NOTTINGHAM

'Trade and Commerce for the Countries provision is frequented in 10 Market-Towns in this Shire, whereof Nottingham is both the greatest and best: a Town seated most pleasant and delicate upon a high hill, for buildings stately, and number of fair streets surpassing and surmounting many other Cities, and for a spacious and most fair Market place doth compare with the best. Many strange Vaults hewed out of the Rocks, in this Town are seen; and those under the Castle of an especial note, one for the story of Christs Passion engraven in the Walls and cut by the hand of David the second King of Scots, whilst he was therein detained prisoner. Another wherein Lord Mortimer was surprised in the non-age of King Edward the third, ever since bearing the name of Mortimers hole; these have their stairs and several rooms made artificially even out of the rocks: as also in that hill are dwelling houses with winding stairs, windows, chimneys, & room above room,

wrought all out of the solid rock. The Castle is strong, and was kept by the Danes against Burthred, Ethelred, and Elfred, the Mercian, and West-Saxon Kings, who together laid their siege against it: and for the further strength of the Town King Edward, surnamed the Elder, walled it about, whereof some parts as yet remains, from the Castle to the West-gate, and thence the foundation may be perceived to the North; where in the midst of the way ranging with this bank, stands a gate of Stone, and the same tract passing along the North part may well be perceived: the rest to the River, and thence to the Castle are built upon, and thereby buried from sight: whose circuit, as I took it, extendeth two thousand one hundred and twenty paces.

In the Wars betwixt Steven and Maud the Empress, by Robert Earl of Gloucester, these Walls were cast down, when also the Town it self suffered the calamity of fire; but recovered to her former estate, hath since increased in beauty and

wealth and at this day is governed by a Mayor and six Aldermen, clad in Skarlet, two Sheriffs, two Chamberlains, a Town-clerk, and six Ser-geants with Maces, their attenders, whose posi-tion hath the pole Elevated Fifty three degrees, twenty five minutes in Latitude, and hath the Meridian 9 degrees, and 25 minutes.'

¶ This fine plan bears easy comparison with the city centre today. The prominent river shown as the 'Leene' (on the county map as 'Lyne') later became part of the Nottingham canal on the south of the city. The River Leen rises at Newstead Abbey and was formerly a small tributary of the Trent, now joining the canal west of the city.

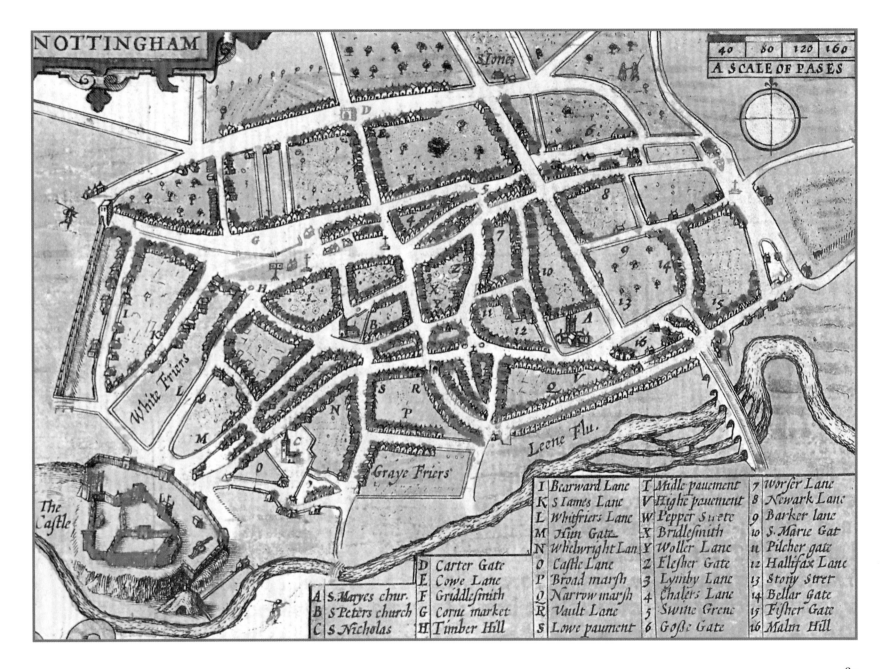

NOTTINGHAM

S Iones

A SCALE OF PASES
40   80   120   160

The Castle

White Friers

Graye Friers

Leene Flu.

A	S. Maryes chur.	D	Carter Gate
B	S Peters church	E	Cowe Lane
C	S Nicholas	F	Griddlesmith
		G	Corne market
		H	Timber Hill

I	Bearward Lane	T	Midle pauement	7	Worser Lane
K	S Iames Lane	V	Highe pauement	8	Newark Lane
L	Whitfriers Lane	W	Pepper Strete	9	Barker lane
M	Hun Gate	X	Bridlesmith	10	S. Marie Gat
N	Whelwright Lan	Y	Woller Lane	11	Pilcher gate
O	Castle Lane	Z	Flesher Gate	12	Hallifax Lane
P	Broad marsh	3	Lymby Lane	13	Stony Stret
Q	Narrow marsh	4	Chalers Lane	14	Bellar Gate
R	Vault Lane	5	Swine Grene	15	Fisher Gate
S	Lowe paument	6	Gosse Gate	16	Malin Hill

89

OAKHAM

'The air is good both for health and delight, subject to neither extremity of heat nor cold, nor is greatly troubled with foggie mists. The Soil is rich, and for Corn and tillage gives place unto none. Woods there are plenty, and many of them imparked, hills feeding heards of Neat, and flocks of sheep, vallies besprinked with many sweet springs, Grain in abundance, and Pastures not wanting: in a word, all things ministered to the content of life, with a liberal heart and open hand. Onely this is objected, that the circuit is not great.

The draught whereof, [Rutlandshire] that I may acknowledge my duty and his right, I received at the hands of the right Honourable John Lord Harrington, Baron of Exton, done by himself in his younger years.

Near unto his house Burley, standeth Okham a fair Market-town, which Lordship the said Baron enjoyeth, with a Royalty somewhat extraordinary which is this: If any Noble by birth come within the precinct of the same Lordship, he shall forfeit as an homage a shooe from the horse whereon he rideth, unless he redeem it at a price with money. In witness whereof, there are many Horse-shooes nailed upon the Shire-Hall door, some of large size and ancient fashion, others new and of our present Nobility. That such homage was his due, the said Lord himself told me; and at that instant a suit depended in Law against the E. of Lincoln, who refused to forfeit the penalty, or to pay his fine.

As this Shire is the least in circuit, so is it with the fewest Market-Towns replenished, having onely two. And from Societies that fed upon the labours of others, was this Land the freest: for besides Rihall, where Tibba the Falconers Goddess was worshiped for a Saint, when Superstition had well-near put Gods true honour out of place, I find very few; neither with more Castles strengthened than that at Okham, whose ruines shew that a Castle hath been there.' 🐝

¶ The quaint story told by Speed of horseshoe 'tolls' in the town, explains the choice of emblem in the town's Arms. The county Arms later adopted the horseshoe as well. As the county town of England's smallest county, then and now, it is pleasing to see it given equal prominence with some of the great cities.

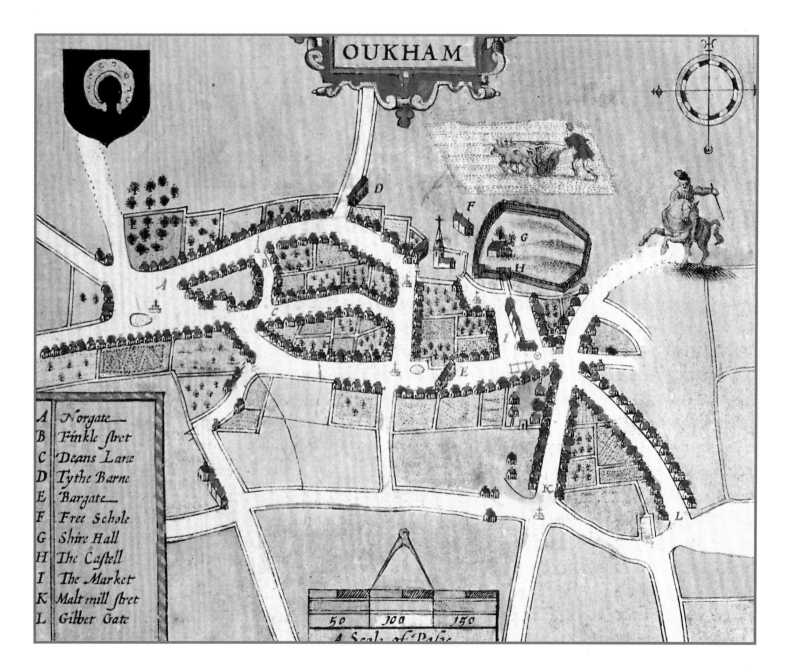

OUKHAM

A	Norgate
B	Finkle ſtret
C	Deans Lane
D	Tythe Barne
E	Bargate
F	Free Schole
G	Shire Hall
H	The Caſtell
I	The Market
K	Malt mill ſtret
L	Gilber Gate

50 100 150

A Scale of Paſe

OXFORD

'This City is, and long hath been, the glorious seat of the Muses, the British Athens, and learnings wellspring, from whose living fountain the wholesome waters of all good literature streaming plenteously, have made fruitful all other parts of this Realm, and gained glory amongst all Nations abroad.

K.Elfred, that learned and religious Monarch, recalled the exiled Muses to their sacred place and built there three goodly Colledges for the Studies of Divinity, Philosophy and other Arts of humanity, sending thither his own son Ethelward, and drew thither the young Nobles from all parts of his Kingdom. From which time that it continued a Seed-plot of Learning till the Norman Conquest, Ingulfus, recordeth, who himself then lived. No marvel then if Mat.Paris called Oxford the second school of Christendom, and the very chief Pillar of the Catholick Church. And in the Council holden at Vienna, it was ordained, that in Paris, Oxford, Bononia, and Salamanca (the only Universities then in Europe) should be erected Schools for the Hebrew, Greek, Arabick and Chaldean tongues, and that Oxford should be the general University for all England, Ireland, Scotland and Wales: which point was likewise of such weight with the Council of Constance, that from this precedence of Oxford University it was concluded that the English Nation was not only to have precedence of Spain in all General Councils, but was also to be held equal with France itself. By which high prerogatives this of ours hath alwaies so flourished, that in the daies of K.Henry the 3d. 30000 Students were therein resident, as Arch-bishop Armachanus (who then lived) hath writ, and Rishanger (then also living) sheweth, that for all the Civil Wars which hindered such places of quiet study, yet 15000 Students were there remaining, whose names (saith he) were entered in Matricula, in the Matriculation Book. About which time, Iohn Baliol (the father of Baliol K.of Scots) built a Colledge, yet bearing his name, Anno 1269. and Walter Merton Bishop of Rochester, that which is now called Merton Colledge; both of them beautified with buildings, and enriched with lands, and were the first endowed Colledges for learning in all Christendom. And at this present there are 16 Colledges (besides another newly builded) with 8 Halls, and many most fair Collegiate Churches, all adorned with most stately buildings, and enriched with great endowments, noble Libraries, and most learned Graduates of all professions, that unless it be her Sister Cambridge, the other nursing breast of this Land, the like is not found again in the world. This City is also honoured with an Episcopal See. As for the site thereof, it is removed from the Equator in the degree 52 and one minute and from the West by Mercator's measure, 19 degrees and 20 minutes.'

¶ The style of engraving differs from most other plans as this plate (Oxfordshire) was not the work of the engraver Jodocus Hondius. The origins of the plan are from a larger original by Ralph Agas surveyed in 1578 and published ten years later. That work showed the city with reversed orientation, i.e. south at the top. Speed has repeated this curiosity, which seems perfectly reasonable as he made no claim of origination.

Chiefe places in the Citie
observed by Alphabetical
letters

A Sainte Giles
B Sainte Johns Colledge
C Trinitie Colledge
D Balliol Colledge
E Magdalaine Chuch
F Saint Michaels
G Iesus Colledge
H Exiter Colledge
I Vniversitie Schooles
K Lincolne Colledge
L All Hallowes
M Saint Martins
N Corne Markett
O St Peters in ye Bailie
P The Castle
Q Saint Thomas
R Saint Ebbes
S Saint Aldates
T Christes Church Col:
V Christes Church
W Corpus Chr: Colledge
X Merton Colledge
Y Saint Maries
Z All Soules Colledge
1 Vniversitie Colledge
2 Brasenose Colledge
3 Oriall Colledge
4 East gate

PETERBOROUGH

'The devotions of the Saxon Kings made Peterborow more famous [than Northampton], formerly called Meddeswel, where Wolphere King of Mercia began a most stately Monastery to the honour of S.Peter, for satisfaction of the blood of his two sons, whom he had murdered in case of Christianity; but himself being for the like made away by his Mother, his Brother Penda continued the work, with the assistance of his Brother Ethelred, and two Sisters, Kineburga and Kineswith. This among the Danish desolations was cast down, yet was it again restored to greater beauty by Ethelwold Bishop of Winchester, with the help of King Edgar, and of Adulph his Chancellor, who upon prick of conscience, that in bed with his wife had overlaid and smothered an infant their only son, laid all his wealth upon the reedifying of the place, and then became Abbot thereof himself. The Cathedral is most beautiful and magnifical, where, in the Quire lie interred two unfortunate Queens: on the North-side Katherine Dowager of Spain, the repudiate wife of King Henry the Eighth, under an Hearse covered with black Say, having a white Cross in the midst: and on the South-side Mary Queen of Scotland, whose Hearse is spread over with black Velvet. The Cloister is large, and in the glass-windows very curiously pourtrayed the History of Wolphere the Founder, whose Royal Seat was at Wedon in the street converted into a Monastery by S.Werburg his holy Daughter, and had been the Roman Station, by Antonine the Emperor called Bannavenna. So likewise Normanchester was the ancient City Durobrivae, where their Souldiers kept, as by the moneys there daily found is most apparent.

Houses of Religion devoted to Gods service by the pious intents of their well-meaning Founders were at Peterborow, Peakirk, Pipewel, Higham, Davintree, Sulby, Sausecomb, Sewardesleg, Gare, S.Dewy, S.Michael, Luffeild, Catesby, Bruch, Barkley, Finshead, Fathringhay, Weedon, and Withrop, besides them in Northampton, all which felt the storms of their own destruction, that raged against them in the Raign of King Henry the Eighth, who dispersed their Revenues to his own Coffers and Courtiers, and pulled the stones asunder of their seeming-sure foundations.'

¶ Dominated by a splendid representation of the cathedral this plan shows how small the city was in 1600. The practice by early mapmakers of using fanciful illustrations to embellish otherwise empty spaces was delightfully epitomised by Swift, who wrote 'So geographers, in Afric maps, with savage pictures fill their gaps…'. On this plan the inclusion (wildly out of scale) of the hare-hunting scene, may have a similar motive.

PETERBOROW

A Borrow Bery
B West gates stret
C Swane Poole
D Bungate
E Bungate hoole
F Sexon Barne
G S.t Iohns
H The Market
I The Prison
K S Peters minst.
L Presgat Lane
M High strete

50   100   150   200

A Scale of ~~miles~~ paces

READING

'When the Romans had rent their own Empire, and retired their Legion into a narrower circuit, the Saxons set foot where their Forces had been, and made this county [Berkshire] a parcel of their Western Kingdom. The Danes then setting their desire upon spoils from their roaving Pinaces pierced into these parts, and at Redding fortified themselves betwixt the Rivers Kennet and Thamisis, whither after their great overthrow received at Inglefield by the hand of King Ethelwolfe, they retired for their further safety.

This Town [Reading] King Henry the first most stately beautified with a rich Monastery and strong Castle, where, in the Collegiate Church of the Abbey, himself and Queen (who lay both veiled and crowned) with their Daughter Maud the Empress, called the Lady of England, were interred, as the private History of the place avoucheth, though others bestow the bodies of these two Queens else-where. The Castle King Henry the Second razed to the ground, because it

was the refuge for the followers of King Stephen. From whence the North pole is raised in Latitude 51 degrees and 40 minutes, and in Longitude from the first West-point observed by Mercator 19 degrees and 35 minutes.

The Air [of Berkshire] is temperate, sweet and delightful and prospect for pleasure inferior to none; the Soil is plenteous of Corn, especially in the Vale of White-horse, that yieldeth yearly an admirable encrease. In a word, for Corn and Cattle, Waters and Woods, of profit and pleasure, it gives place unto none.

The Riches and sweet Seats that this County affordeth, made many devout persons to shew their devotions unto true piety, in erecting places for Gods Divine Service, and their exemptions from all worldly business: such were Abington, Redding, Bisham, Bromehall, Henley, Hamme, and Wallingford, whose Votaries abusing the intents of their Founders, overthrew both their own Orders and places of Professions, all which

were dissolved by Act of Parliament, and given the King to dispose at his will.'

¶ As with a few other plans, Reading does not appear on the correct map (Berkshire), but is shown on Buckinghamshire. Speed explains this rather disarmingly in a cartouche beside the plan saying 'For that Barkshire cold not contayn place for this Towne I have here inserted it …'. In fact the Berkshire map is dominated by a panoramic view of Windsor Castle leaving no space for town plans or heraldry. The plan of Reading includes pastoral aspects such as milking and some high-spirited livestock.

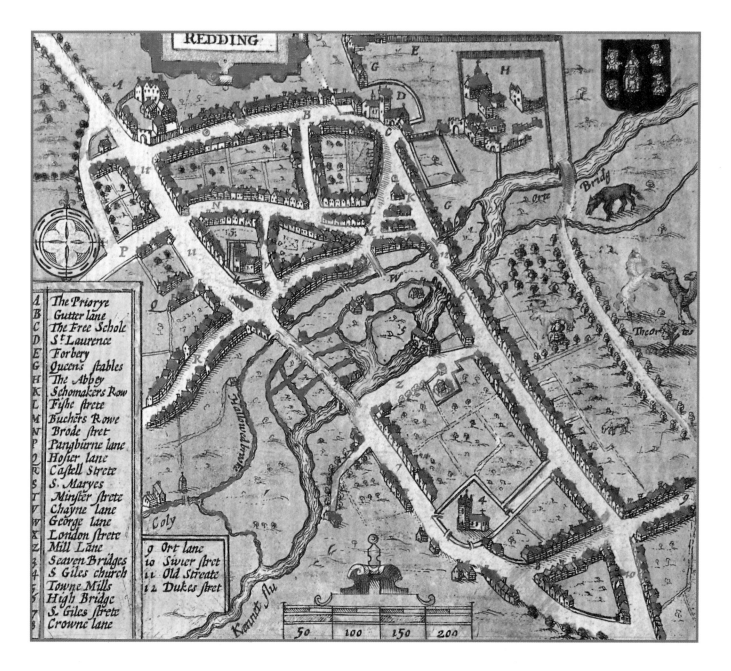

REDDING

A	The Priorye
B	Gutter lane
C	The Free Schole
D	St Laurence
E	Forbery
G	Queens stables
H	The Abbey
K	Schomakers Row
L	Fyshe strete
M	Buchers Rowe
N	Brode stret
P	Pangburne lane
Q	Hosier lane
R	Castell Strete
S	S. Maryes
T	Minster strete
V	Chayne lane
W	George lane
X	London strete
Z	Mill Lane
3	Seaven Bridges
4	S Giles church
5	Towne Mills
6	High Bridge
7	S Giles strete
8	Crowne lane

9	Ort lane
10	Siuer stret
11	Old Streate
12	Dukes stret

Coly

Kennet flu

50   100   150   200

RICHMOND

'Richmond the chief Town of the North Riding, seated upon Swale, seemed to have been fenced with a wall, whose gates yet stand in the midst of the Town, so that the Suburbs are extended far without the same. It is indifferently populous and well frequented, the people most imployed in knitting of Stockings, wherewith even the decrepit, and children, get their own livings.

Alan the first Earl thereof, distrusting the strength of Gilling (a Mannor house of his not far off, called by Bede Gethling) to withstand the violence of the Danes and English, whom the Normans had despoiled of their inheritance, built this Town, and gave it the name, calling it Richmond, as one would say, The Rich Mount, which he fortified with a Wall and strong Castle set upon a Rock: for Gilling ever since the time of Oswy K.of Northumberland (being there guestwise entertained) was murtherously made away, was more regarded in respect of Religion then for any strength it had: in expiation of which Murther, the Monastery was founded and had in great account among our Ancestors. This Town for the administration of government, hath an Alderman yearly chosen out of twelve Brethren, who is assisted by twenty four Burgesses, a Recorder, four Chamberlains, and two Sergeants at Mace. The position of this place for Latitude is set in the degree 55,17 minutes from the North Pole, and for Longitude from the first West-point in the degree 18, and 50 minutes.

Things of rarity and worthy observation in this County, are those hills near Richmond, where there is a Mine or Delf of Copper mentioned in a Charter of King Edward the fourth, having not as yet been pierced into. Also, those Mountains, on the top whereof are found certain stones much like unto Sea-winkles, Cockles, and other Sea fish; which if they be not the wonders of nature, yet with Orosius (a Christian Historiographer) we may deem to be the undoubted tokens of the general deluge that in Noahs time overflowed the whole face of the earth. Also the River Swale (spoken of before) which among the ancient English was reputed a very sacred River, and celebrated with an universal glory, for that (the English Saxons first embracing Christianity) in one day above ten thousand men, besides a multitude of women and children, were therein baptized unto Christ, by the hands of Paulinus Archbishop of York: A holy spectacle when out of one Rivers channel so great a progeny sprung up, for the celestial and heavenly City.'

¶ The lofty situation of Richmond is not readily apparent from this plan, although the shading between the castle walls and the river gives some impression of elevation. The very large open market place in the town centre was as apparent then as it is now.

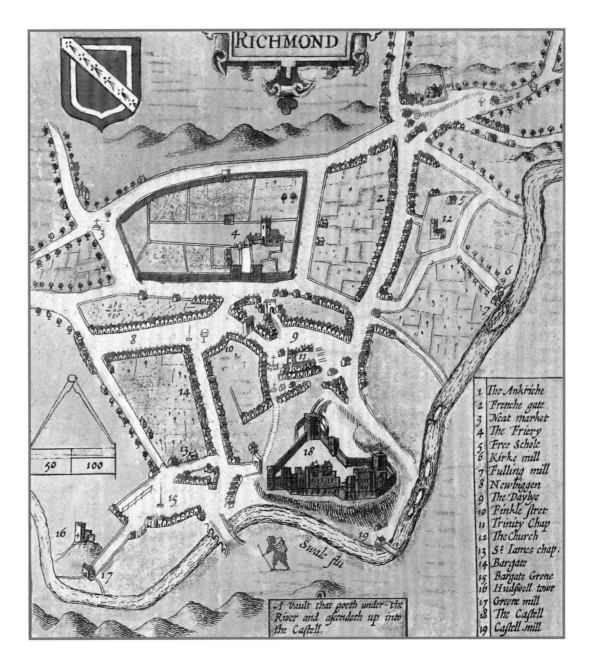

RICHMOND

1 The Ankriche
2 Frenche gate
3 Neat market
4 The Friery
5 Free Schole
6 Kirke mill
7 Fulling mill
8 Newbiggen
9 The Daylye
10 Finkle stret
11 Trinity Chap
12 The Church
13 St Iames chap:
14 Bargate
15 Bargate Grene
16 Hudswell towr
17 Greene mill
18 The Castell
19 Castell mill

Swale flu

A vault that goeth under the
River and ascendeth up into
the Castell.

50   100

ROCHESTER

'Rochester (as Beda saith) was built by one Rof, Lord of the same, though some ascribe the foundation of the Castle to Julius Caesar, and hath been often ruinated by the injuries of War, both in the times when the Saxons strove for superiority among themselves, wherein this City was laid wast, anno 680 as also in the assaults of their common enemy the Danes, who about the year 884 from France sailed up the River Medway, and besieged the same, so that had not King Elfred speedily come to the rescue, it had been overthown by those Pagans. And again, in an.999 the Danes miserably spoiled this City in the time of King Ethelred; neither hath it stood safe from danger since (though not defaced so much by war) for twice hath it been sore endamaged by chance of fire: the first was in the Reign of King Henry I. anno 1130 himself being present with most of his Nobility, for the Conse-cration of the Cathedral Church of St.Andrew. And again almost wholly consumed about the latter end of the Reign of King Henry II. anno 1177. Yet after all these calamities it recovered some strength againe, by the bounty of King Henry III. both in buildings, and it ditching her about for defence.

Sundry navigable Rivers are in Kent, whereof Medwey, that divides the Shire in the midst, is chief; in whose bosom securely rideth his Majestys Navy Royal, the Walls of the Land and terrors of the Seas; besides ten others of name and account, that open with 20 Creeks and Havens for Ships arivage into this Land, four of them bearing the name of Cinque Ports, are places of great strength and priviledges, which are Dover, Sandwich, Rumney and Winchelsey: among which Dover with the Castle is accounted by Matth. Paris, the Monk, the Lock and Key to the whole Realm of England; and by John Rosse and Lidgate is said to be built by Julius Caesar fatal only for the death of K.Stephen, and surrender of K.John therein hapning.

The Kentish people in Caesars time were accounted the civillest among the Britains: and as yet esteem themselves the freest Subjects of the English, not conquered, but compounded with by the Normans: and herein glory that the King and Commons of all the Saxons were the first Christians, converted in ann.596 yea and long before that time also Kent received the Faith: for it is recorded that Lucius the first Christian British King in this Island, built a Church to the name and service of Christ in the Castle of Dover endowing it with the Toll of the same Haven.'

¶ The town plan of Rochester incorporated into Speed's map of Kent is simple and lacking the detail which is typical of nearly all the other town plans. It omits a key and a 'Scale of Paces', and is clearly not by Speed himself. It appears to have been copied from a plan published in the late 16th century.

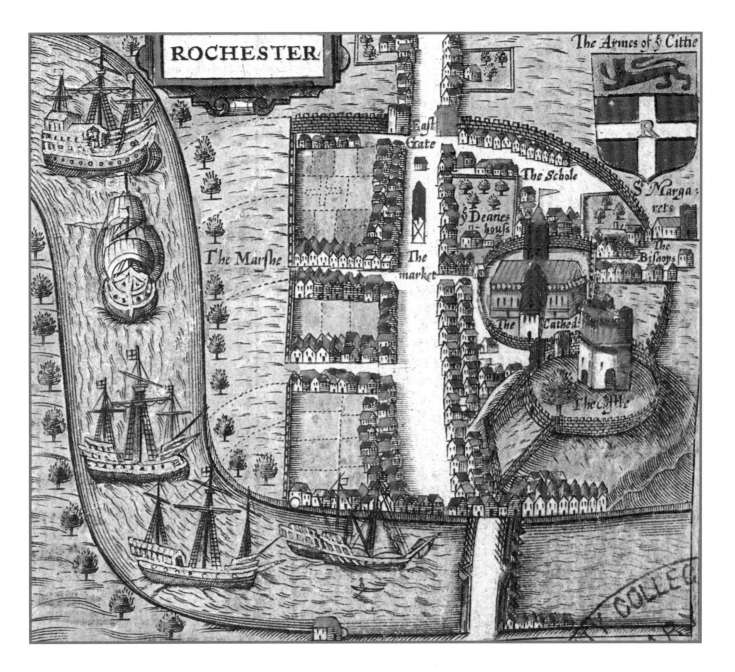

ROCHESTER

The Armes of ý Cittie

East Gate

The Schole

St Deanes hous

St Marga rets

The Marshe

The market

The Cathed

The Bishops

The Castle

SALISBURY

'The chiefest City of this Shire [Wiltshire] is Salisbury, removed from a higher, but a far more convenient place; whose want of water was not so great in the mother as is supplied and replenished in the daughter, every street almost having a River running thorow her midst; and for sumptuous and delicate buildings is inferior to none.

The Cathedral, a most rich magnificent Church, was begun by Richard Poore, Bishop, and forty years continuance was raised to her perfect beauty, wherein are as many Windows as there are daies in the year, as many cast Pillars of Marble as there are hours in the year and as many Gates for entrance as there are moneths in the year.

Neither doth this City retain true honour to her self, but imparteth hers, and receiveth honour from others, who are entitled, Earls of Salisbury, whereof eight Noble Families have been dignified since the Normans Conquest, and is now enjoyed by that most wise and loyal Counsellor Robert Cecil, Lord high Treasurer of England, and the worthy Patron of the place whereof myself am a member. This Cities situation is in the degree of latitude 51,10 minutes; and from the first West-point observed by Mercator, 18 degrees, and 31 minutes of longitude.

For air, it [Wiltshire] is seated in a temperate Climate, both sweet, pleasing and wholesome; and for soil (saith John of Sarisbury) is exceeding fertile and plentiful, yea, and that with variety. The Northern part, which they call North-Wiltshire, riseth up into delectable Hills attired with large Woods and watered with cleer Rivers, whereof Isis is one, which soon becometh the most famous in the land. The South part is more even, yielding abundantly grass and corn and is made the more fruitful by the Rivers Wily, Adder and Avon. The midst of this county is most plain, and thereby is known and commonly Salisbury Plains; and lies so level indeed, that they do limit the Horizon; for hardly can a man see from the one side to the other. These Plains graze an infinite number of sheep whose fleeces and flesh bring in an yearly revenue to their owners.'

¶ Speed's map of Wiltshire is among his finest and most interesting. The plan of Salisbury has considerable detail, and remarkably true representations of the main buildings, particularly the Cathedral. Just west of Salisbury the village of North Burcombe was shown on Speed's map as 'Quaere' and this error was repeated by numerous other mapmakers for the next hundred years, despite their claims of completely new surveys etc. The explanation is undoubtedly that a query was noted on the proof, either by Speed or by the Dutch engraver, and never corrected. This has become a celebrated talking-point over the years.

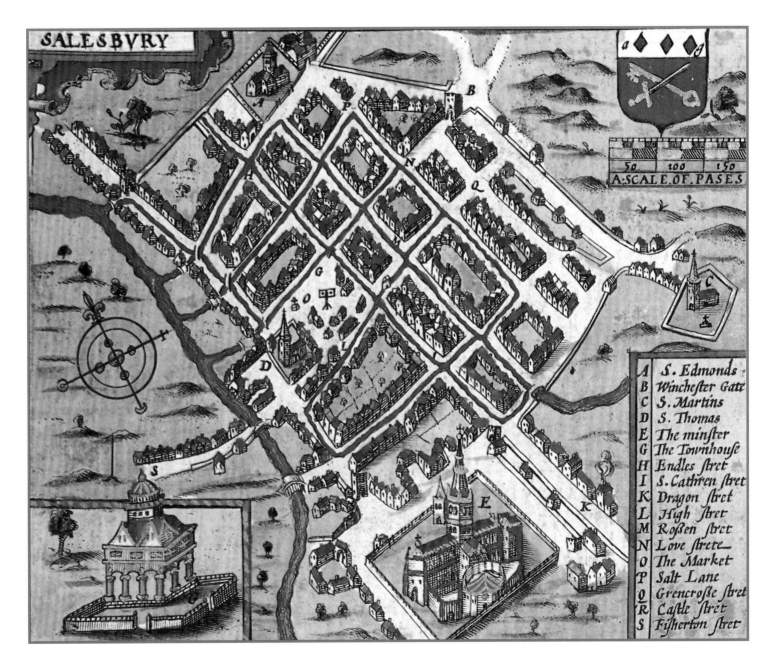

SALESBVRY

A:SCALE:OF:PASES
50   100   150

A	S. Edmonds
B	Winchester Gate
C	S. Martins
D	S. Thomas
E	The minster
G	The Townhouse
H	Endles stret
I	S. Cathren stret
K	Dragon stret
L	High stret
M	Rossen stret
N	Love strete
O	The Market
P	Salt Lane
Q	Grencrosse stret
R	Castle stret
S	Fisherton stret

SHREWSBURY

'This being the Marches of England and Wales, was sore afflicted by bloody broils, which caused many of their Towns to be strongly walled, and thirty two Castles to be strongly built: lastly, into this County the most wise King Henry the seventh sent his eldest Son Prince Arthur, to be resident at Ludlow, where that fair Castle became a most famous Princes Court. And here King Henry the eighth ordained the Counsel of the Marches, consisting of a Lord President, as many Counsellors as the Prince shall please, a Secretary, an Attorney, a Solicitor, and four Justices of the Counties in Wales, in whose Court were pleaded the causes depending, and termly tried for the most part in presence of that honourable President.

But the Shire-town Shrewsbury, for circuit, trade and wealth, doth far exceed this, and is inferior to few of our Cities; her Buildings fair, her Streets many and large, her Citizens rich, her Trade for the most part in the staple commodities of Cloth and Friezes; her walls strong, and of a large compass, extending to seventeen hundred paces about, besides another Bulwark ranging from the Castle, down unto and in part along the side of Severn; thorow which there are three entrances into the Town, East and West over by two fair stone-Bridges, with Towers, Gates and Bars; and the third into the North, no less strong than them, over which is mounted a large Castle, whose gaping chinks do doubtless threaten her fall. This Town is governed by two Bayliffs, yearly elected out of twenty four Burgesses, a Recorder, Town-Clerk, and Chamberlain, with three Sergeants at Mace: the Pole being raised hence from the degrees of Latitude 53,16 minutes; and from West in Longitude 17 degrees, 27 minutes.

Wholsome is the Air, delectable and good, yielding the Spring and the Autumn, Seed-time and Harvest in a temperate condition, and affordeth health to the inhabitants in all seasons of the year. The soil is rich, and standeth most upon a reddish clay, abounding in wheat and Barly, Pit-coals, Iron and Woods, which two last continue not long in league together. It hath Rivers that make fruitful the Land, and in their waters contain great store of fresh fish, whereof Severn is the chief, and second in the Realm, whose stream cutteth this County in the midst, and with many windings sporteth her self forward, leaving both Pastures and Meadows bedecked with flowers and green colours, which every where she bestoweth upon such her attendants.'

❦

❡ One of the strangest of Speed's town plans. It seems to be a mixture of bird's-eye view and overhead plan. The perspective is particularly incongruous just below the scale where the enclosures almost overlay the hilly views. The northernmost part of the town also contrasts strangely with the hills on either side. Despite this it is still a fine representation of a town that clearly impressed John Speed.

KEY

A	Colam Bridg
B	Stone Bridg
C	Under the wyle
D	WyleCapp
E	Dogg Pole
F	Almes houses
G	Saint Maryes
H	High Paument
K	Scholhouse lane
L	North Gate
M	The Lords place
N	S. Maryes waterlod
O	Castle foregate
P	Pintle Broke
Q	The Shambles
R	Fishe Strete
S	Grope Lane
T	Milk Strete
V	Beche Lane
W	St. Chads Almesho
Y	Saint Chads
X	Kyll Lane
Z	The Colledge
1	Stery Close Lane
2	Market house
3	Hey Strete
4	The Stales
5	Shomakers Row
7	Meryvauce
8	St. Iohns hill
10	Hound Stret
11	Cleryman hill
12	Backer stret
14	Mard Wall
15	Rousehill Lane
17	Rousehill
18	Knoken Stret
19	Carnarvan Lane
20	Criples Lode
22	St. Aulkemans chu.
23	St. Iulians Church
24	Welsh Bridge

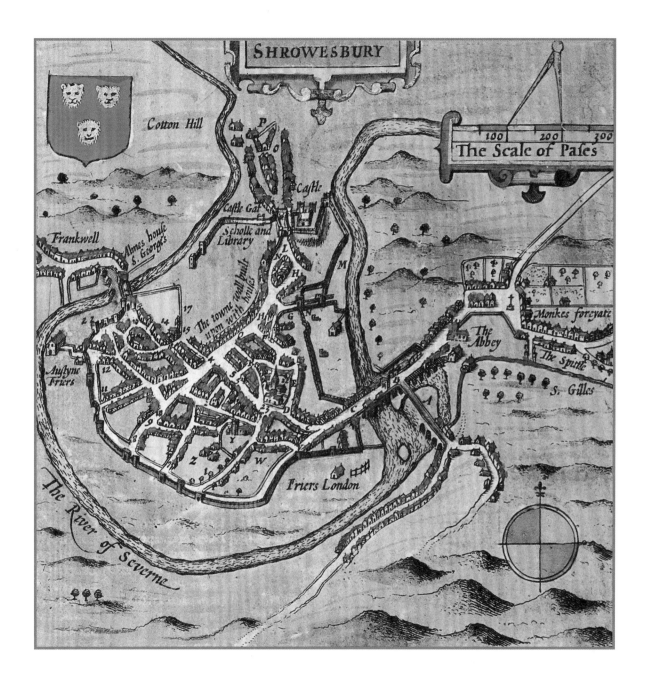

SOUTHAMPTON

'More South, [than Winchester] is Southampton, a Town populous rich and beautiful, from whom the whole Shire deriveth her name, most strongly walled about with square stone, containing in circuit, 1200 paces, having seaven Gates for entrance, and 29 Towres for defence, two very stately Keys for Ships arrivage, and five fair Churches for Gods divine service, besides an Hospital called Gods house, wherein the unfortunate Richard, Earl of Cambridge, beheaded for treason, lieth interred.

On the West of this Town is mounted a most beautiful Castle, in form Circular, and wall within wall, the foundation upon a hill so topped, that it cannot be ascended but by stairs, carrying a goodly prospect both by Land and Sea, and in the East without the walls a goodly Church sometimes stood, called S.Maries, which was pulled down, for that it gave the French direction of course, who with fire had greatly endangered the Town instead thereof, is now newly erected a small and unfinished Chappel. In this place sayeth learned Cambden, stood the ancient Clausentium, or fort of the Romans, whose circuit on that side extended it self to the Sea: this suffered many depredations by the Saxon Pirates, and in An.980 was by the Danes almost quite overthrown. In King Edward the thirds time, it was fired by the French, under the Conduct of the King of Sicils son, whom a Countryman encountred and struck down with his Club. He crying Rancon, that is, Ransome: but neither understanding his language, nor the Law that Armes doth allow, laid on more soundly, saying, I know thee a Frankon, and therefore shalt thou die: and in Richard the seconds time it was somewhat removed, and built in the place where now it standeth. In this Clausentium Canute to evict his flatterers, made trial of his Deitie, commanding the Seas to keep back from his seat: but being not obeyed, he acknowledged God to be the only supream Governor, and in a religious devotion gave up his Crown to the Rood at Winchester.

The general commodities gotten in this Shire are Wools, Cloths, and Iron, whereof store is therein wrought from the Mines, and thence transported into all parts of this Realm, and their Cloths and Karsies carried into many forraign Countries, to that Countries great benefit, and Englands great praise.'

¶ This town plan did not appear on Speed's map of Hampshire through lack of space, and was instead included on the Isle of Wight map. The plan is undoubtedly his own work and well balanced. Speed's descendants became important figures in Southampton during the late 17th and 18th centuries.

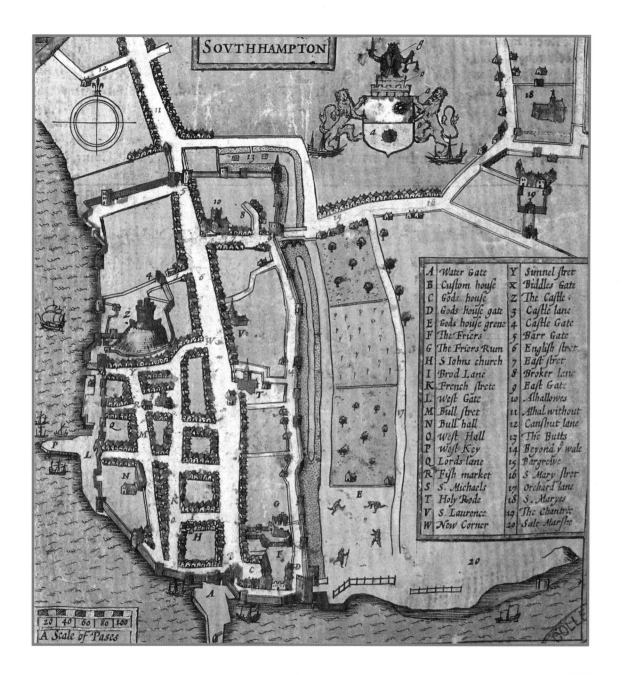

STAFFORD

'Stafford the Shire Town, anciently Betheney, from Bertelin, a reputed holy man that therein lead an Hermits life, was built by King Edward the elder, incorporated by King John, and upon the East and South part was walled and trenched by the Barons of the place; the rest from East to North was secured by a large Pool of water, which now is become fair Meadow grounds. The tract and circuit of these walls extended to 1240 paces, thorow which four Gates into the four winds have passage, the River Sowe running on the South and West of the Town.

King Edward the sixth did incorporate the Burgesses, and gave them a perpetual succession, whose Government is under two Bayliffs yearly elected out of one and twenty Assistants, called the Common Counsel, a Recorder, whereof the Dukes of Buckingham have born the Office, and as yet is kept a Court of Record wherein they hold Plea without limitation of summ; a Town Clerk also, (from whose Pen I received these instructions) and to attend them two Sergeants at Mace. This Town is sited in the degree of latitude 53,20 scruples, and of longitude 18, and 40 scruples.

The Commodities of this County consist chiefly in Corn, Cattel, Alablaster, Woods and Iron (if the one prove not the destruction of the other) Pit-coal, flesh and fish, whereof the River Trent is said to swarm: and others arising and running thorow this Shire do so batten the ground, that the Meadows even in the midst of Winter grow green; such are Dowe, Manifold, Churnot, Hunsy, Yenden, Yean, Blith, Trent, Tyne, and Sowe; whereof Trent is not only the principal, but in esteem accounted the third of this Land

The Air is good, and very healthful, though over-sharp in her North and Moreland, where the Snow lieth long, and the wind bloweth cold. The Soil in that part is barren of Corn, because her Hills and Mores are no friends unto Tillage: the middle is more level, but therewithal wooddy, as well witnesseth that great one called the Cank. But the South is most plenteous in Corn and Pasturage.'

¶ The vignette above the town is particularly pleasing and the ploughman is nicely complemented by the fisherman shown in the lower right-hand corner. The town does not appear to be very important or prosperous, and Speed's brief description seems to confirm this impression.

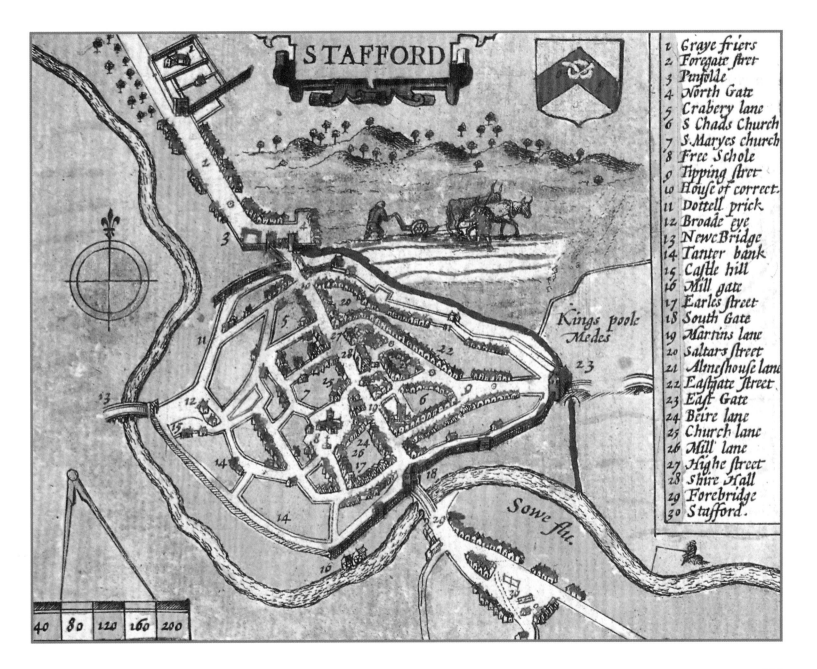

STAFFORD

1. Graye friers
2. Foregate ſtret
3. Penſolde
4. North Gate
5. Crabery lane
6. S Chads Church
7. S. Maryes church
8. Free Schole
9. Tipping ſtret
10. Houſe of correct.
11. Dottell prick
12. Broade eye
13. Newe Bridge
14. Tanter bank
15. Caſtle hill
16. Mill gate
17. Earles ſtreet
18. South Gate
19. Martins lane
20. Saltars ſtreet
21. Almeshouſe lane
22. Eaſtgate ſtreet
23. Eaſt Gate
24. Beire lane
25. Church lane
26. Mill lane
27. Highe ſtreet
28. Shire Hall
29. Forebridge
30. Stafford.

Kings poole Medes

Sowe flu.

40 80 120 160 200

STAMFORD

'Let it not seem offensive, that I (to fill up this little Shire) have inserted the seat of a Town [Stamford] not sited in this County; for besides the conveniency of place, the circuit and beauty, but especially it being for a time an University, did move much; yea and the first in this Island if John Hardings Author fail him not, that will have Bladud to bring from Athens certain Philosophers, whom here he seated, and made publick profession of the Liberal Sciences, where (as he sayeth) a great number of Scholars studies the Arts, and so continued an University unto the coming of Augustine, at which time the Bishop of Rome interdicted it; for certain Heresies sprung up among the Britains and Saxons. But most true it is, that in the raign of King Edward the third, upon debate falling betwixt the Southern and Northern Students at Oxford, many School-men with-drew themselves hither, and a while professed, and named a Colledge, according to one in Oxford, Brazen-Nose, which retaineth that name unto this day. This was so great a skar unto the other, that when they were recalled by Proclamation to Oxford, it was provided by Oath, that no student in Oxford should publickly profess or read the Arts at Stanford, to the prejudice of Oxford.

The Shires [Lincolnshire] Commodities consist chiefly in Corn, Cattle, fish, Fowl, flax and Alabaster; as also in a Plaister much esteemed of by the Romans for their works of Imagery; and whereof Pliny in his natural History maketh mention. And the Astroites, a precious stone, star-like, pointed with five beams or rays, anciently esteemed for their virtue in victories, upon the South-west of this County near Bever are found; not far thence in our Fathers memory, at Harlaxton was ploughed up a brasen vessel, wherein was inclosed a golden Helmet of an ancient fashion, set with precious stones, which was presented to Katherin of Spain, Wife and Dowager to King Henry the eight.' ❧

¶ The town is so close to the Rutland border, though in Lincolnshire, that it is quite natural for it to be included in the Rutland map, and Speed is typically straightforward about this in his narrative. The notation in the key reverses the omission of figures 1 and 2, found elsewhere, and instead omits the letters I and Z, to avoid confusion.

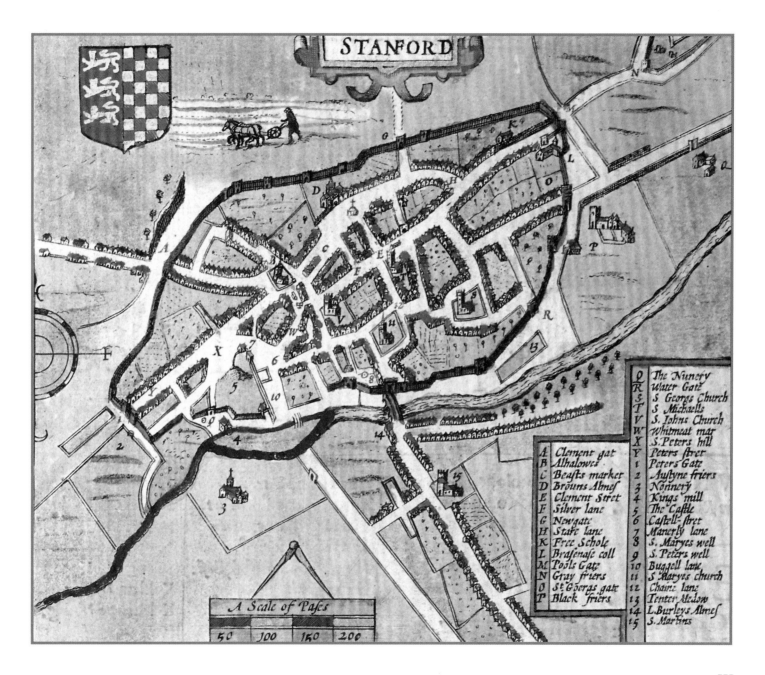

STANFORD

A Scale of Paces

50 100 150 200

A	Clement gat
B	Alhalowes
C	Beasts market
D	Brouns Almes
E	Clement Stret
F	Silver lane
G	Newgate
H	Stafe lane
K	Free Schole
L	Brasenase coll
M	Pooles Gate
N	Gray friers
O	St Goeras gate
P	Black friers

Q	The Nunery
R	Water Gate
S	S. Georges Church
T	S. Michaells
V	S. Iohns Church
W	Whitmeat mar
X	S. Peters hill
Y	Peters stret
1	Peters Gate
2	Austyne friers
3	Nonnery
4	Kings mill
5	The Castle
6	Castell-stret
7	Manerly lane
8	S. Maryes well
9	S. Peters well
10	Buggell lane
11	S. Maryes church
12	Chaine lane
13	Tenter Medow
14	L. Burleys Almes
15	S. Martins

III

WARWICK

'Next unto this City [Coventry], in account and Commerce is Warwick, upon the Norwest-bank of Avon, built by Gurgunstus the son of Beline, as John Rosse, Monk of the place, sayeth, 375 years before the birth of Christ: by Ninius called Caer-Guarvic and Caer-Leon; by the Saxons, Wappyng-wyc; and by learned Cambden judged to be PRAESIDIUM, the Roman Garisons Town. The situation of this place is most pleasant, upon a hill rising from the River, over which is a strong and fair Stone-bridge, and her sharp storm upon the Town side checked with a most sumptuous and stately Castle, the decaies whereof, with great cost and curious buildings, the right worthy Knight Sir Foulke Grivel (in whose person shineth all true vertue and high nobility) hath repaired; whose merits to me-ward I do acknowledge, in setting this hand free from the daily imployments of a manual Trade, and giving it full liberty thus to express the inclination of my mind, himself being the Procurer of my present estate.

It seemeth this Town hath been walled about, as appeareth by the Trench in some places seen, and two very fair Gates, whose passages are hewed out of the Rock, as all other into the Town are; over whom two beautiful Chappels are built; that towards the East called S.Peters and that on the South-west, S.James.

Two fair Churches are therein seated, called S.Maries, and S.Nicholas; but these in and about the Town suppressed, S.Laurence, S.Michaels, John Baptist, and John of Jerusalem, besides the Nunnery in the North of the Town; whose North Pole is elevated in Latitude 52 degrees 45 minutes, and is seated from the first point in the West of Longitude, 18 degrees, and 45 minutes, being yearly governed by a Bayliff, twelve Brethren, twenty four Burgesses for Common-Council, a Recorder, a Town Clerk, and one Sergeant there attendant.

At Leamington, so far from the Sea, a Spring of Salt-water boileth up; and at Newenham Regis most soveraign water against the Stone, Green wounds, Ulcers, and Imposthumes; and drunk with Salt looseth but with Sugar bindeth the body; and turneth wood into stone as my self saw by many sticks that therein were fallen, some part of them Ash, and some part of them Stone.'

¶ This plan was by Speed, identifying only half as many locations as on the Coventry Plan, which is more to do with their relative size than any lack of zeal by Speed in his survey. Indeed it seems that he would have liked more landmarks to be named as his key includes a final reference number (14) left blank.

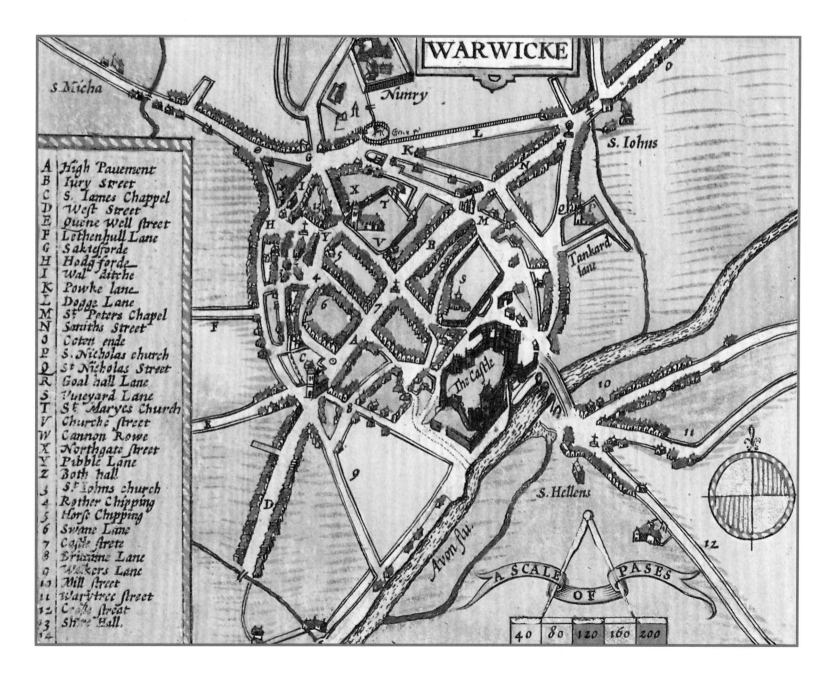

WARWICKE

A	High Pauement
B	Iury Street
C	S. Iames Chappel
D	West Street
E	Quene Well street
F	Lethenhull Lane
G	Saktesforde
H	Hodg forde
I	Wal ditche
K	Powke lane
L	Dogge Lane
M	St Peters Chapel
N	Smiths Street
O	Coten ende
P	S. Nicholas church
Q	St Nicholas Street
R	Goal hall Lane
S	Vineyard Lane
T	St Maryes Church
V	Churche street
W	Cannon Rowe
X	Northgate street
Y	Pibble Lane
Z	Both hall
3	St Iohns church
4	Rother Chipping
5	Horse Chipping
6	Swane Lane
7	Castle strete
8	Brianine Lane
9	Walkers Lane
10	Mill street
11	Warytree street
12	Crosse streat
13	Shire Hall
14	

s. Micha

Nunry

S. Iohns

S. Hellens

Tankard lane

The Castle

Avon flu.

A SCALE OF PASES

| 40 | 80 | 120 | 160 | 200 |

WESTMINSTER

¶ [*continued from that of London*]: 'This London (as it were) disdaining bondage, hath set herself on each side, far without the Walls, and left her Westgate in the midst, from whence with continual buildings (still affecting greatness) she hath continued her Streets unto a Kings Palace, and joyned a second City [Westminster] to her self, famous for the Seat and Sepulchre of our Kings; and for the Gates of Justice, that termly there are opened, only once a Bishops See, whose Title dyed with the man. No Walls are set about this City, and those of London are left, to shew rather what it was, than what it is: whose Citizens, as the Lacedemonians did, do repose their strength in their Men, and not in their Walls, how strong soever. Or else for their multitude, cannot be circulated, but (as another Jerusalem) is inhabited without Walls, as Zachary said. The Wealth of this City (as Isay once spake of Nilus) grows from the Revenues and Harvest of her South-bounding Thames; whose Traffick for Merchandising is like that of Tyrus, whereof Ezechiel speaks, and stands in abundance of Silver, Iron, Tyn and Lead, &c. And from London the Channel is navigable, straitened along with medowing borders, until she taketh her full liberty in the German Seas. Upon this Thamesis the Ships of Tharsis seem to ride, and the Navy, that rightly is termed the Lady of the Sea, spreads her sail. Whence twice with lucky success hath been accomplished the compassing of the universal Globe.

This River Canutus, laying siege against London, sought by digging to divert, and before him the Danes had done great harms in the City, yet was their State recovered by King Elfred, and the Rivers kept her old course, notwithstanding that cost. In the times of the Normans some civil broils have been attempted in this City, as in the days of King John, whereinto his Barons entred, and the Tower yielded unto Lewis, And again, Wat Tyler herein committed outragious cruelties, but was worthily stook down by the Mayor and slain in Smithfield. This Cities graduation for Latitude is the degree 51. 45 minutes, and in Longitude 20 degrees, 39 minutes.'

¶ Then as now, the cities of London and Westminster were seamlessly joined and both had been surveyed for plans published some years before by Braun and Hogenburg. The north orientation of the Westminster plan is incorrect and probably copied, unchecked, from the earlier source.

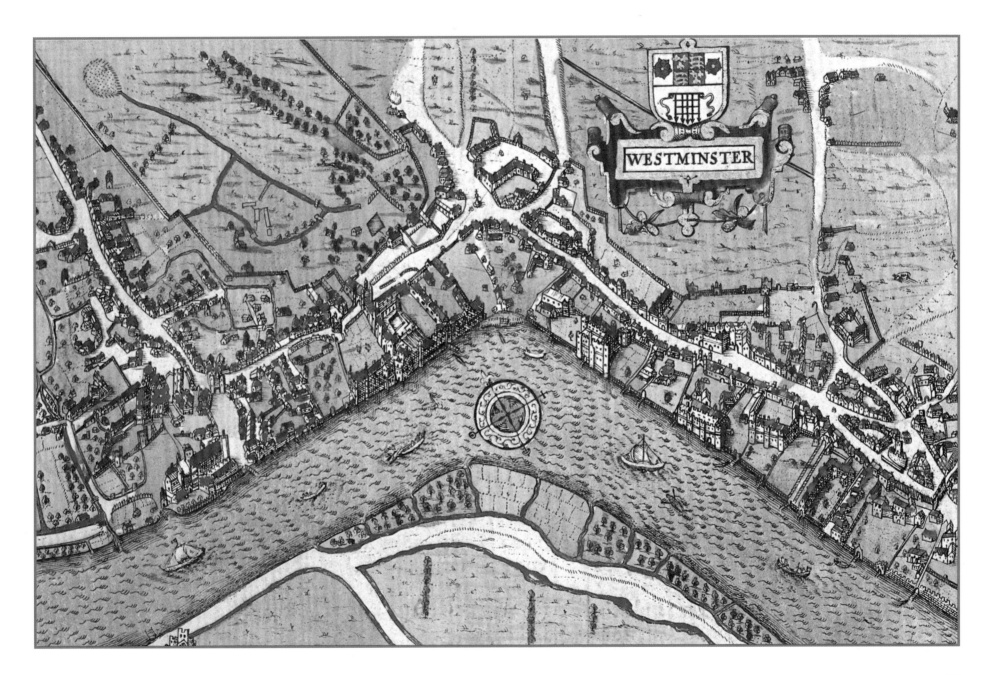

WINCHESTER

'There are eighteen Market Towns in this Shire [Hampshire], whereof Winchester, the Britains Caer Gwent, the Romans Venta Belgarum, and the Saxons Windonearden is chief, ancient enough by our British Historians, as built by King Rudhudibras, nine hundred years before the Nativity of Christ: and famous in the Romans times for the weavings and embroideries therein wrought, to the peculiar uses of their Emperours own persons. In the Saxons time, after two Calamities of consuming fire, her walls were raised, and the City made the Royal Seat of their West Saxons Kings, and the Metropolitan of their Bishops See, wherein Egbert and Elfred their most famous Monarchs were crowned: and Henry the third, and Normans longest reigner first took breath: and here King Athelstane erected six houses for his Mint: but the Danish desolation over-running all, this City felt their fury in the days of King Ethelbright, and in the Normans time, twice was defaced by the misfor-

tune of fire, which they again repaired and graced with the trust of keeping the publike Records of the Realm. In the civil Wars of Maud and Stephen, this City was sore sacked, but again receiving breath, was by King Edward the third appointed the place for Mart of Wool and Cloth. The Cathedral Church built by Kenwolf King of the West Saxons that had been Amphibalus, S.Peters, Swithins, and now holy Trinity, is the Sanctuary for the ashes of many English Kings: for herein great Egbert, An.836 with his Son King Ethelwolfe, 857. Here Elfred Oxfords founder 901. with his Queen Elswith 904. Here the first Edmund before the Conquest 924 with his sons Elfred and Elsward: Here Edrid 955 and Edwy, 956, both Kings of England: Here Emme, 1052, with her Danish Lord Canute, 1035.and his son Hardicanute, 1042. And here lastly the Normans, Richard and Rufus 1100 were interred; their bones by Bishop Fox were gathered and shrined in little guilt coffers fixed upon a wall in the

Quire, where still they remain carefully preserved.

This Cities situation is fruitful and pleasant, in a vally under hils, having her River on the East, and Castle on the West, the circuit of whose walls are well near two English miles, containing 1880 paces; thorow which openeth six gates for entrance, and therein are seaven Churches for divine service, besides the Minster, and those decayed: such as Callendar, Ruell Chappel, S.Maries Abbey and the Fryers, without in the Suburbs, and Sooke; in the East is S.Peters, and in the North Hyde-Church and Monastery, whose ruines remaining, shew the beauty that formerly it bare. The Graduation of this City by the Mathematicks, is placed for Latitude in the degree 51,10 minutes, and for Longitude 19,3 minutes.'

❡ Although the plan of Winchester on the Speed map of Hampshire is smaller than most, due to space constraints, it still shows the whole city as surveyed by Speed. The representation of St Kathrens Hill, on the right of the plan, is a typical sugar-loaf which Speed used throughout his maps to show hills and mountains. Contour lines were not developed until the 18th century.

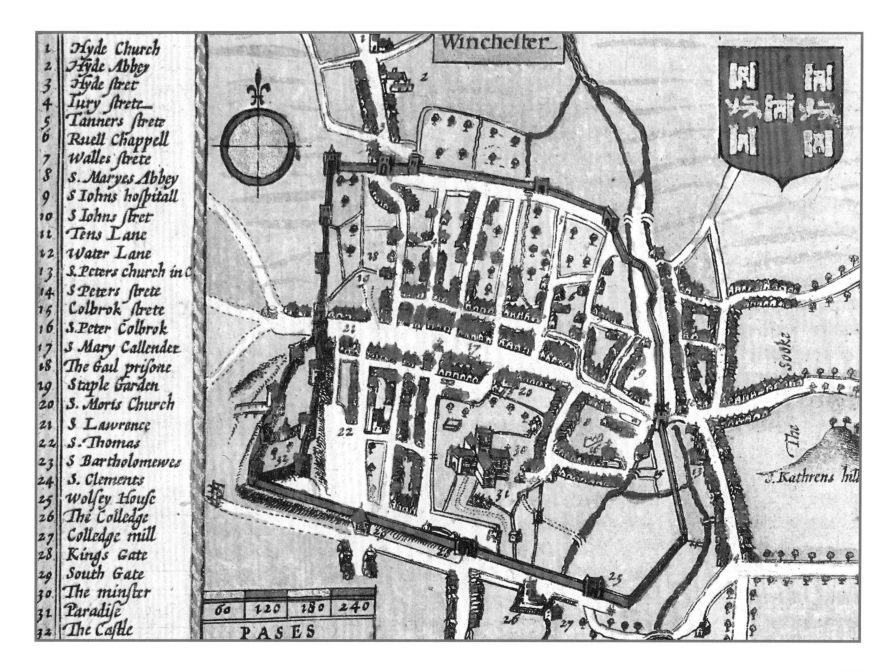

1	Hyde Church
2	Hyde Abbey
3	Hyde ſtret
4	Iury ſtrete
5	Tanners ſtrete
6	Ruell Chappell
7	Walles ſtrete
8	S. Maryes Abbey
9	S Iohns hoſpitall
10	S Iohns ſtret
11	Tens Lane
12	Water Lane
13	S. Peters church in C
14	S Peters ſtrete
15	Colbrok ſtrete
16	S. Peter Colbrok
17	S Mary Callender
18	The Gail priſone
19	Staple Garden
20	S. Moris Church
21	S Lawrence
22	S. Thomas
23	S Bartholomewes
24	S. Clements
25	Wolſey Houſe
26	The Colledge
27	Colledge mill
28	Kings Gate
29	South Gate
30	The minſter
31	Paradiſe
32	The Caſtle

Wincheſter

PASES

60   120   180   240

The Sooke

The J. Kathrens hill

WORCESTER

'True it is that the County doth hold the name from her chief City Worcester. Which is most pleasantly seated, passing well frequented, and very richly inhabited. This was the Branonium mentioned by Antonine and Ptolemy, called by the Britains, Caer-wrangon; by Ninius, Caer-gurcon: by the old Saxons, Wine-ceardon: and by the Latins, Vigornia. This City is seated upon the East-bank of Severn, and from the same is walled in triangle wise about, extending in circuit one thousand six hundred and fifty paces: thorow which seven Gates enter, with five other Watch-Towers for defence. It is thought the Romans built this to restrain the Britains that held all beyond Severn. This City by Hardy Canute in the year of Christ 1041 was sorely endangered and set on fire, and the Citizens slain almost every one, for that they had killed his Collector of the Danish Tribute: yet was it presently repaired and peopled, with many Burgesses, and for fifteen Hides discharged it self to the Conqueror, as in his Doomesdaies is to be seen. But in the year 1113 a sudden fire hapned, no man knew how, which burnt the Castle and Cathedral Church. Likewise in the civil broils of King Stephen it was twice lighted into a flame and the later laid it hopeless of recovery. Notwithstanding from those dead ashes a new Phoenix arose, and her building raised in a more stately proportion, especially the Cathedral dedicated to S.Mary, first laid by Bishop Sexwolf, in Anno 680; since when it hath been augmented almost to the River: In the midst of whose Quire, from his many turmoils, resteth the body of King John (the great withstander of the Popes proceedings) under a Monument of white Marble, in Princely Vestures, with his portraiture thereon according to life. And in the South-side of the same Quire lieth intombed Prince Arthur the eldest Son to King Henry the seventh; his Monument is all black Jett, without remembrance of him by picture.

This City is governed by two Bailiffs, two Aldermen, two Chamberlains, and two Constables yearly elected out of 24 Burgesses clothed in Scarlet assisted with 48 other Citizens, whom they call their Common Counsellors, clad in Purple, a Recorder, Town-Clerk, and five Sergeants with Mace, their Attendants. Whose Geographical position is distant in longitude from the West-Meridian 18 degrees, 10 scruples, having the North-pole elevated in latitude 52 degrees, and 32 scruples.'

¶ This pleasant plan includes the arms of the city, and clearly marked are the Heraldic French key letters indicating the colours. This was a device used throughout the atlas (and later atlases by other cartographers) and was essential for amateur colourists. The key letters are:- A for 'argent' (silver), B for 'bleu' (blue), G for 'gules' (red), O for 'or' (gold), P for 'pourpure' (purple), S for 'sable' (black) and V for 'verte' (green).

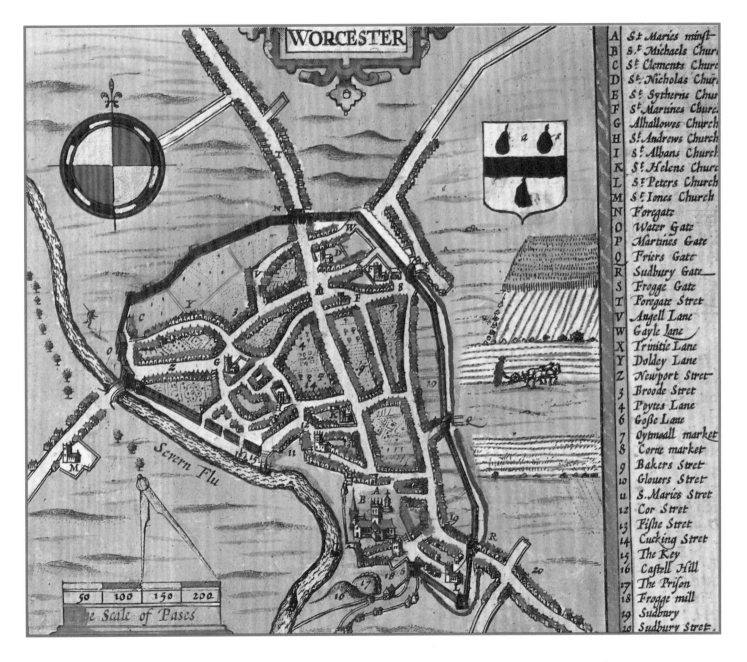

WORCESTER

A	St. Maries minst
B	St. Michaels Chur
C	St. Clements Chur
D	St. Nicholas Chur
E	St. Sytherne Chur
F	St. Martines Church
G	Alhallowes Church
H	St. Andrews Church
I	St. Albans Church
K	St. Helens Chur
L	St. Peters Church
M	St. Iones Church
N	Foregate
O	Water Gate
P	Martines Gate
Q	Friers Gate
R	Sudbury Gate
S	Frogge Gate
T	Foregate Stret
U	Angell Lane
W	Gayle Lane
X	Trinitie Lane
Y	Doldey Lane
Z	Newport Stret
3	Broode Stret
4	Poytes Lane
6	Goße Lane
7	Oytmeall market
8	Corne market
9	Bakers Stret
10	Glouers Stret
11	S. Maries Stret
12	Cor Stret
13	Fishe Stret
14	Cucking Stret
15	The Key
16	Castell Hill
17	The Prison
18	Frogge mill
19	Sudbury
20	Sudbury Stret

Severn Flu

50 100 150 200

The Scale of Pases

YORK

'I will forbear to be prolix or tedious in the particular memoration of places in a Province [Yorkshire] so spacious, and only make a compendious relation of York, the second City of England, in latine called Eboracum.

It over-masters all the other places of this country [county] for fairness, and is a singular ornament and safeguard to all the North parts. A pleasant place, large & full of magnificence, rich, populous, and not only strengthened with fortifications, but adorned with beautiful buildings as well private and publick. For the greater dignity thereof it was made an Episcopal See by Constantius, and a Metropolitan City by a Pall sent unto it from Honorius. Egbert Archbishop of York who flourished about the year seven hundred forty, erected in it a most famous Library. Richard the third repaired the Castle thereof being ruinous, and King Henry the Eighth appointed a Counsel in the same, to decide and determine all the causes and Contro-

versies of the North-parts, according to equity and conscience: which Counsel consisteth of a Lord President, certain Counsellors at the Princes pleasure, a Secretary, and other under Officers.

The original of this City cannot be fetcht out but from the Romans, seeing the Britains before the Romans came, had no other towns then woods fenced with trenches and rampiers: as Caesar and Strabo do testifie.

Howbeit Athelstane recovered it from the Danish subjection, and quite overthrew the Castle with which they had fortified it; yet was it not (for all this) so freed from Wars, but that it was subject to the times fatally next following. Nevertheless in the Conquerors time, when (after many woful overthrows and troublesom storms) it had a pleasant calm of ensuing peace, it rose again of it self, and flourished afresh, having still the helping hand both of Nobility and Gentry, to recover the former dignity, and bring it to the perfection it hath: The Citizens fenced it round

with new walls, and many towers and bulwarks, and ordaining good and wholesome laws for the government of the same. Which at this day are executed at the command of a Lord Mayor, who hath the assistance of twelve Aldermen, many Chamberlains, a Recorder, a Town Clerk, six Sergeants at Mace, and two Esquires, which are, a Swordbearer and the Common Sergeant, who with a great Mace goeth on the left hand of the Sword. The longitude of this City, according to Mercator's account is 19 degrees and 35 scruples, the latitude 54 degrees and 40 scruples.'

¶ York at the second millennium still has more of its nearly 2000 year history in evidence than any other English city. The city centre within the mediaeval walls has so little changed in the past 400 years that a copy of John Speed's plan could be used today with confidence. Virtually all of the important buildings identified by him still exist, dominated by perhaps Europe's finest Cathedral.

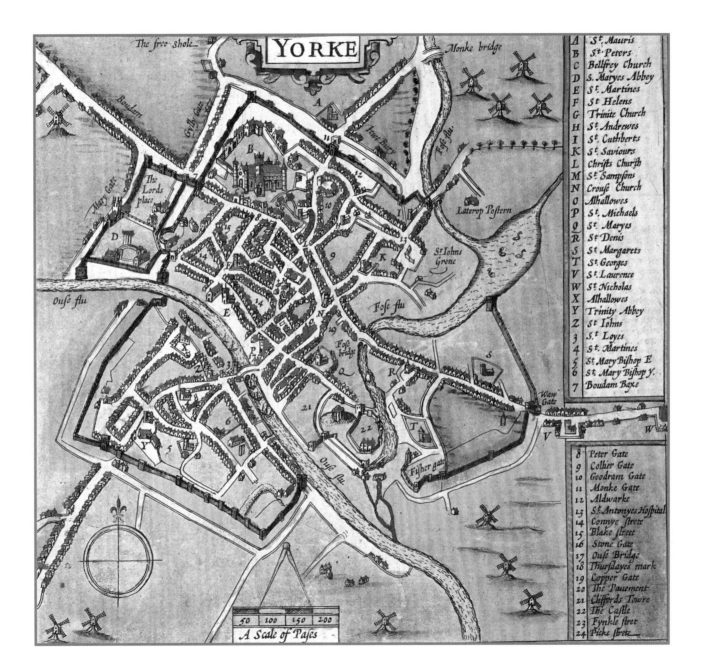

YORKE

The free shole

Monke bridge

A St. Mauris
B St. Peters
C Bellfrey Church
D S. Maryes Abbey
E St. Martines
F St. Helens
G Trinite Church
H St. Andrewes
I St. Cuthberts
K St. Saviours
L Christs Church
M St. Sampsons
N Crouse Church
O Athallowes
P St. Michaels
Q St. Maryes
R St. Denis
S St. Margarets
T St. Georges
V St. Laurence
W St. Nicholas
X Alhallowes
Y Trinity Abbey
Z St. Iohns
3 St. Loyes
4 St. Martines
5 St. Mary Bishop E
6 St. Mary Bishop Y.
7 Boudam Baxe

8 Peter Gate
9 Collier Gate
10 Goodram Gate
11 Monke Gate
12 Aldwarke
13 St. Antonyes Hospital
14 Connye strete
15 Blake strete
16 Stone Gate
17 Ouse Bridge
18 Thursdayes mark
19 Copper Gate
20 The Pauement
21 Cliffords Towre
22 The Castle
23 Fynkle stret
24 Picke stret

The Lords place

St. Iohns Grene

Laterop Postern

Ouse flu

Fose flu

Fose bridge

Wam Gate

Fisher gate

Ouse flu

50 100 150 200

A Scale of Paces

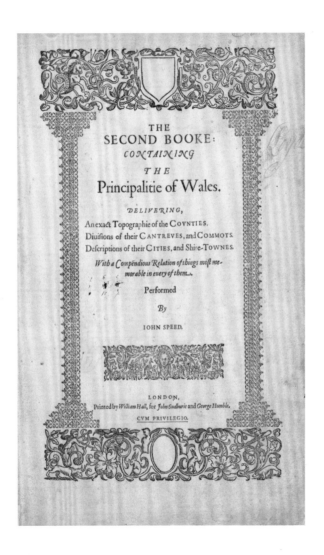

THE
SECOND BOOKE:
CONTAINING
THE
Principalitie of Wales.

DELIVERING,

An exact Topographie of the COVNTIES.
Diuisions of their CANTREVES, and COMMOTS.
Descriptions of their CITIES, and Shire-TOWNES.

With a Compēndious Relation of things most memorable in euery of them.

Performed

By

IOHN SPEED.

LONDON,
Printed by *William Hall*, for *John Sudburie* and *George Humble*.
CVM PRIVILEGIO.

The Welsh Town Plans

BANGOR

'Bangor the Bishops See, though it be now but a small Town, yet was it in times past so large, that for the greatness thereof it was called Banchor Vaur, that is Great Banchor, which Hugh Earl of Chester fortified with a Castle: But it hath been long since utterly ruinated and laid level with the ground, insomuch as there is not any footing to be found or other monuments left thereof, although they have been sought with all diligent enquiry. This Bishops See hath within the Diocess ninety six Parishes. But the ancient Church which was consecrated unto Daniel, somtime Bishop thereof, was defaced and set on fire by that notorious Rebel, Owen Glendowerdwy, who had a purpose also to destroy all the Cities of Wales, for that they stood for the King of England. And though the same Church was since repaired about the time of King Henry the seventh, yet hath it scarce recovered the resemblance of her former dignity.

The soil cannot be much commended for the fertility, except those parts of the Sea-coasts, which lie on the West toward Ireland: but for the heart of this Shire, it is altogether mounainous, as if nature had a purpose here, by rearing up these craggy hills so thick together, strongly to compact the joynts of this our Island, and to frame the Inland part thereof for a fit place of refuge to the Britains against those times of adversity which afterward did fall upon them; for no army though never so strongly, or scarce any Travellers, though never so lightly appointed, can find passage among those so many rough and hard Rocks, so many Vales, and Pools here and there, crossing all the ways, as ready obstacles to repel any Inrodes of foreign assailants. These Mountains may not unfitly be termed the British Alps, as being the most vast of all Britain and for their steepness and cragginess not unlike those of Italy, all of them towering up into the air, and round encompassing one far higher then all the rest, peculiarly called Snowdon-hill, though the other likewise in the same sense, are by the Welsh termed Craig Eriry, as much as Snowy Mountains, taking their name as doth (by Pliny's testimony) Niphates in Armenia, and Imaus in Sythia: For all the year long these lie mantled over with Snow hard crusted together, though otherwise for their height they are open and liable both to the Sun to dissolve them, and the winds to oversweep them.'

¶ This simple plan, one of the two on the Caernarvonshire map, indicates a modest town which did not compare favourably with Caernarvon either in size or apparent well-being at that time. It is nevertheless an integral part of the most appealing of Speed's Welsh maps.

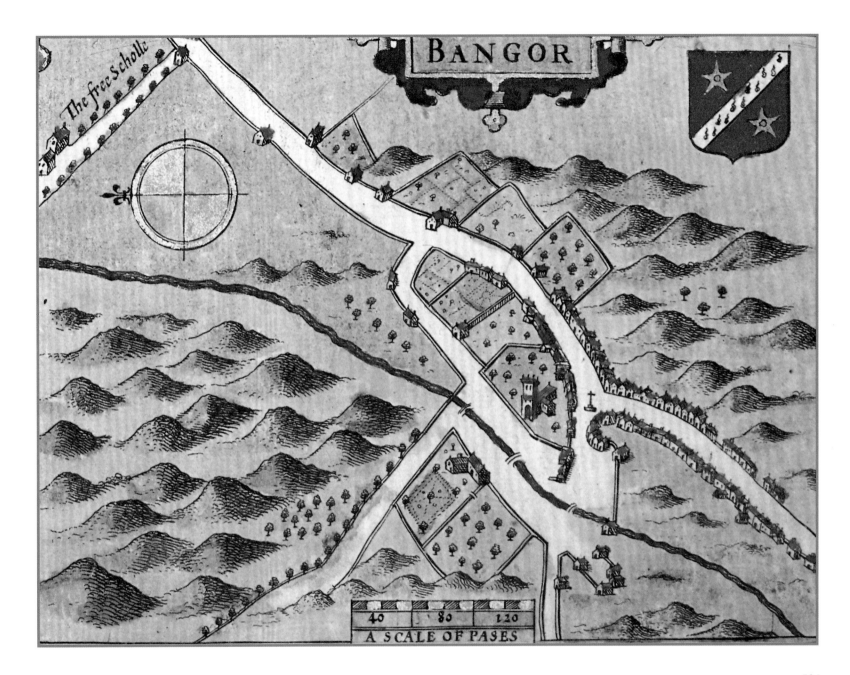

The free Scholle

BANGOR

40   80   120
A SCALE OF PASES

125

BEAUMARIS

'The principal Town in this Isle [Anglesey] is Beau-marish, which the said King Edward the first built in the East-side thereof, and for the fair situation, though in a Moorish place, gave it the name which it now beareth, whereas in times past it was called Bonouer, which he also fortified with a goodly Castle.

The Mayor is the chiefest Magistrate of the Town, who is yearly chosen, and hath the assistance and help of two Bailiffs, two Sergeants at Mace, and one Town-Clerk: by whose careful diligence the affairs of this Town are orderly managed and commanded: whose latitude is 54. and longitude 15, 45 minutes.

Anglesey was in the time of the Romans called Mona, by the Britains Mon and Tier-Mon (that is) the Land of Mon, of the ancient English-Saxons Moneg:

And at last, after the Englishmen had by their sharp and several assaults brought it under their rule, and became Lords thereof, it was termed Anglesey, as one would say, The Englishmens Island.

For, an Island it is, albeit it be severed from the Continent of Britain, but with a small and narrow strait of the River Menai, and on all other parts beaten upon with the surging and troublous Irish Sea, in which it lieth somewhat squarewise, not much different in length and bredth; being, where it reacheth out in length, from Beaumarish East-ward, to the utmost Promontory Westward, which we call Holy-Head, twenty miles, and in bredth from Llanbederick North-ward, to the point of Menai South-ward, seventeen miles; the whole circuit or circumference amounting to-wards seventy miles.

The air is reasonable grateful and healthful, and not generally subject to diseases, excepting certain Agues at some times, which are occasioned by the fogs and misty exhalations, which arise from the Sea called Mare Virginium, with the which this Isle is encompassed.' 🐾

¶ Another of Speed's best plans with all the features that make them so appealing as well as revealing. The addition of local residents in the sea gives further charm to the depiction of this small but pleasant resort.

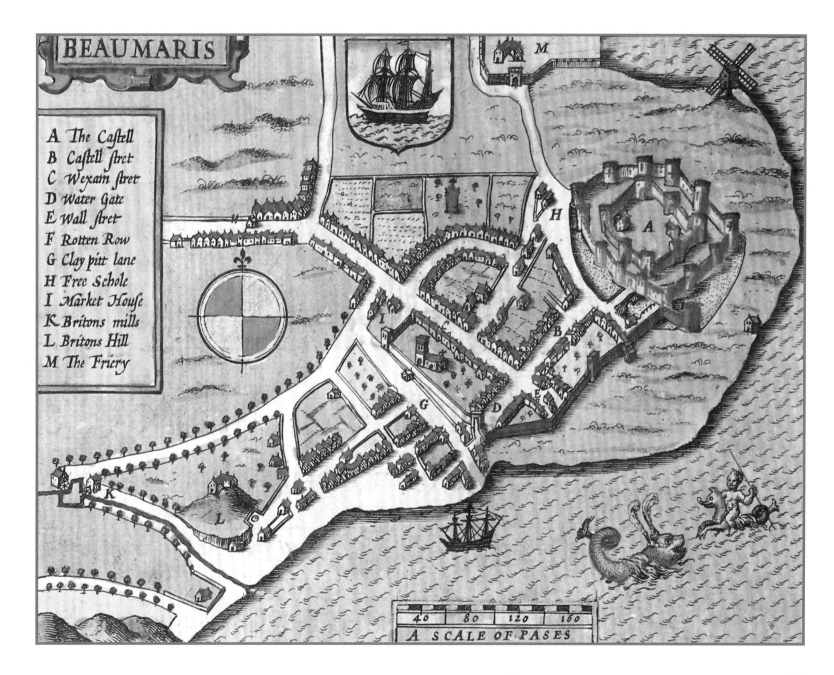

BEAUMARIS

A The Castell
B Castell stret
C Wexam stret
D Water Gate
E Wall stret
F Rotten Row
G Clay pitt lane
H Free Schole
I Market House
K Britons mills
L Britons Hill
M The Friery

A SCALE OF PASES

40   80   120   160

127

BRECON

'Brecknock the Shire-Town, for buildings and beauty retaineth a much better regard, whose walls in Oval-wise are both strong and of good repair, having three Gates for entrance, with ten Towers for defence and is in circuit six hundred and forty paces, upon whose West part a most sumptuous and stately Castle is seated, the like wherof is not commonly seen, whose decays approaching do increase her ruines daily and in the end is feared will be her fall.

This Town is seated upon the meeting of two Rivers, Houthy and Usk, whose yearly government is committed to two Bailiffs, fifteen Aldermen, two Chamberlains, two Constables, a Town-Clerk, and two Sergeants their attendants: having the Poles elevation in 52.21 minutes of Latitude, and for Longitude is placed in the 16. and 32 minutes, as the Mathematicians do measure them.

A mountain in the South, three miles from Breck-nock, is of such height and operation, as is uncredible: and were it not that I have witness to affirm what I shall speak, I should blush to let the report thereof pass from my pen: In my perambulations in these parts, remaining in Brecknock to observe the site of that town, the Aldermen or chief Seniors thereof regarding my pains, with friendly and courteous entertainments at my departure, no less then eight of them, that had been Bailiffs of the Town, came to visit me; where they reported upon their credit and trials, that from the top of that hill, in the Welch called Mounch-denny, or Cadier Arthur, they had oftentimes cast from them and down the North-East Rock, their Cloaks, Hats, and Staves, which notwithstanding would never fall, but were with the air and wind still returned back, and blown up: neither, said they, would any thing descend from that Cliff being so cast, unless it be stone or some metalline substance: affirming the Cause to be the Clouds which are seen to rack much lower then the top of that hill.' ❧

¶ This small but detailed plan has all the features of Speed's best work and is most pleasing. The delightful first-hand account of dramatic events on a nearby hill, in his second paragraph, refers to 'Monuchdenny Hill' which is shown on the county map as an enormous double sugar-loaf, larger than that for Snowdon shown on the map of Caernarvonshire.

It is possible that John Speed spent more time per town in Wales than he did in English towns. This may have been because travel in the wilds was hazardous, and once having arrived he made the most of it. He generally writes more personally and with greater enthusiasm in his narrative of the principality.

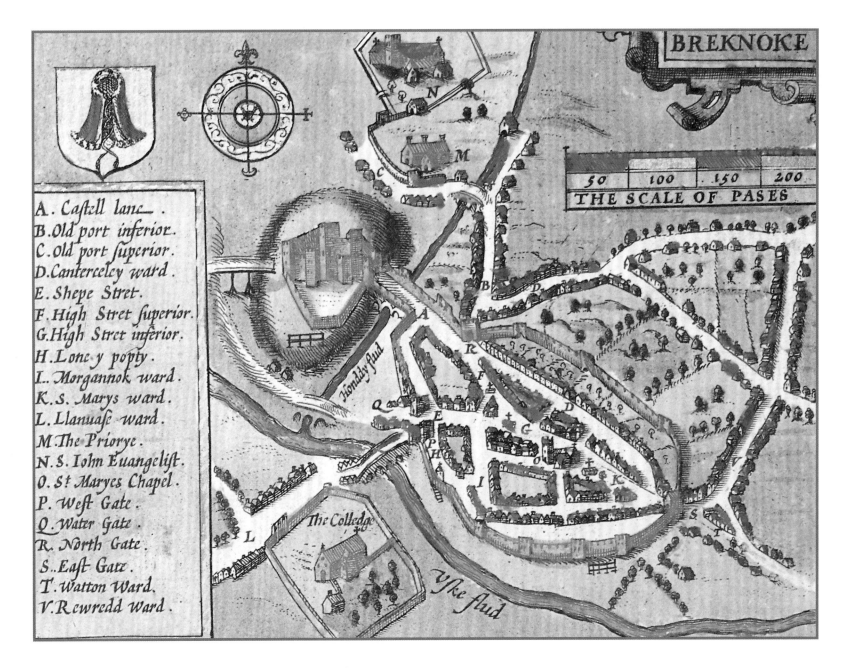

BREKNOKE

THE SCALE OF PASES

50   100   150   200

A. Castell lane.
B. Old port inferior.
C. Old port superior.
D. Canterceley ward.
E. Shepe Stret.
F. High Stret superior.
G. High Stret inferior.
H. Lone y popty.
I. Morgannok ward.
K. S. Marys ward.
L. Llanuase ward.
M. The Priorye.
N. S. Iohn Euangelist.
O. St Maryes Chapel.
P. West Gate.
Q. Water Gate.
R. North Gate.
S. East Gate.
T. Watton Ward.
V. Rewredd Ward.

Honddy flud

The Colledge

Vske flud

129

CAERNARVON

'Touching places of note, that City is very ancient which the Emperour Antonine called Segontium, taking name of a River running by, which at this day is called Seiont: some relicks of the walls whereof do yet appear, near unto a little Church consecrated to the honour of Saint Publicius. This City Ninnius called Caer Custenith, which some interpret the City of Constantine. Indeed Matthew Westminster saith (how true I know not) that Anno 1283 hear was found the body of Constantius (Father to great Constantine) which King Edward the first caused to be sumptuously bestowed in the Church of the new City, which he raised out of the Ruins of the old, and is now called Caernarvon, which giveth name to this whole Shire. The Town it self yieldeth a most excellent prospect towards the Sea, and is incompassed (in a manner) round with the walls of the Castle: so as we may say, it is a City within a Castle, which taketh up the whole West-side of it: and great pity it is, that so famous a work should not be perpetuous, or ever become the ruine of time, which is much feared, for the merciless underminings of the Sea, that with her daily and forcible irruptions, never ceaseth to wash away the foundations of the key. The people of this Town are well approved for courtesie and also civil government, which is administred by the Constable of the Castle (who is ever Mayer by Patent) having the assistance of one Alderman, two Bailiffs, two Sergeants at Mace, and one Town-Clerk. The Townsmen do not a little glory that King Edward the second was born there, in a Tower of the Castle called Eagle-tower, and surnamed of Caernarvon, he being the first Prince of Wales of the English line. The site of this Town, according to Mathematical observation, is in the degree of Longitude 15, & 50 scruples from the first West-point and the Pole elevated in Latitude 53, and 50.' 🐎

¶ This is an excellent plan of an important and thriving town, showing much detail and some marine life. The map of Caernarvonshire is one of Speed's most striking and attractive, and certainly the best of the Welsh maps. The plans of Caernarvon and Bangor are embellished with elaborate strapwork and provide fine balance for the county map. The contrast between the two towns is

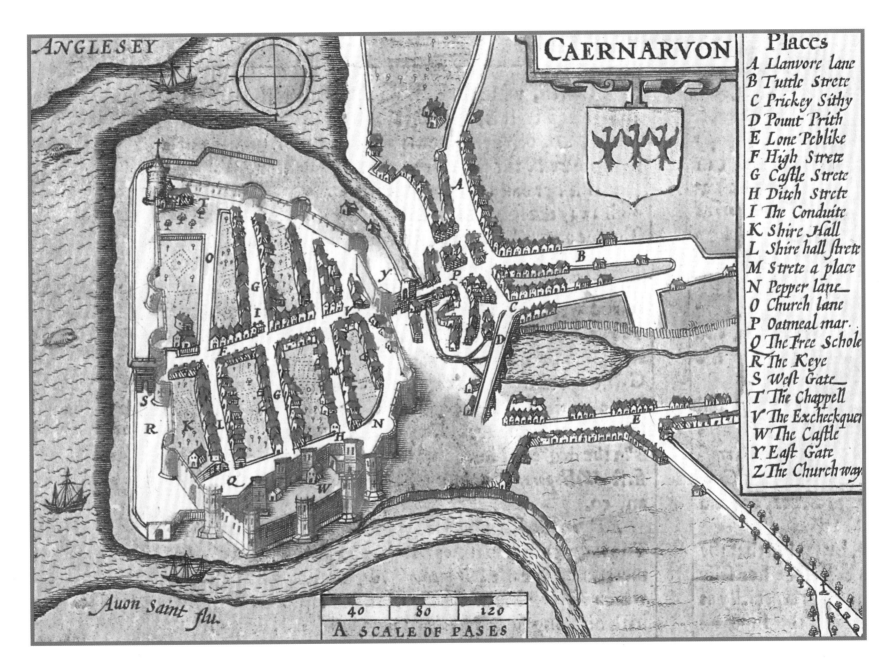

ANGLESEY

CAERNARVON

Places
A Llanvore lane
B Tuttle Strete
C Prickey Sithy
D Pount Prith
E Lone Peblike
F High Strete
G Castle Strete
H Ditch Strete
I The Conduite
K Shire Hall
L Shire hall strete
M Strete a place
N Pepper lane
O Church lane
P Oatmeal mar.
Q The Free Schole
R The Keye
S West Gate
T The Chappell
V The Excheckquer
W The Castle
Y East Gate
Z The Church way

Auon Saint flu.

40   80   120
A SCALE OF PASES

CARDIFF

'Upon whose fall [the River Tave i.e. Taff], and East-bank the fairest Town of all South-Wales is seated, the Britains Caerdid, the English Caerdiff, which fitz-haimon fortified with a Wall and a Castle, in the reign of King Rufus, when he and his Norman Knights had overcome Rhese the Prince of these parts, and thrust out Jestine from his lawful possession. This Town he made his own seat and Court of Justice, enjoyning his Consorts to give aid to this honour, and to hold their portions in vassalage of him.

Strong was the Castle, as by the Trust therein reposed may well appear, where the youngest Brother, Beauclark kept captive the eldest Curthose, both of them Sons of the Conqueror, the space of twenty six years. This Castle is large, and in good repair, whence the Town-wall went both South and East to the Rivers side, through which four Gates enter into the four winds, and contain in compass nine hundred and twenty paces; and along the River (a sure defence) upon her West side, three hundred more; so that the Town containeth in circuit twelve hundred and fourscore paces. But as the Tave is a friend to the Town, in making a Key for arrivage of shipping, so is she a foe to S.Maries Church in the South, with undermining her foundations, and threatning her fall.

The Town is governed by a Mayor yearly elected out of twelve Aldermen, assisted with other twelve Burgesses, a Town-Clerk, four Constables, and two Serjeants with Mace; whose sight is observed from the North-Star to lie in the degree of Latitude 51.and 49 scruples; and from the first point in the West 16.and 52 scruples.'

¶ There is further illustration on this plan of the arbitrary approach to spelling in Speed's time. The title of the Glamorgan map shows 'Cardyff', the body of the map shows 'Cardif', and the plan gives a further variation, yet they all appear on the same engraved copperplate. As this was produced in Holland perhaps we can blame the Dutch engraver, though proof-checking was clearly not undertaken very carefully either.

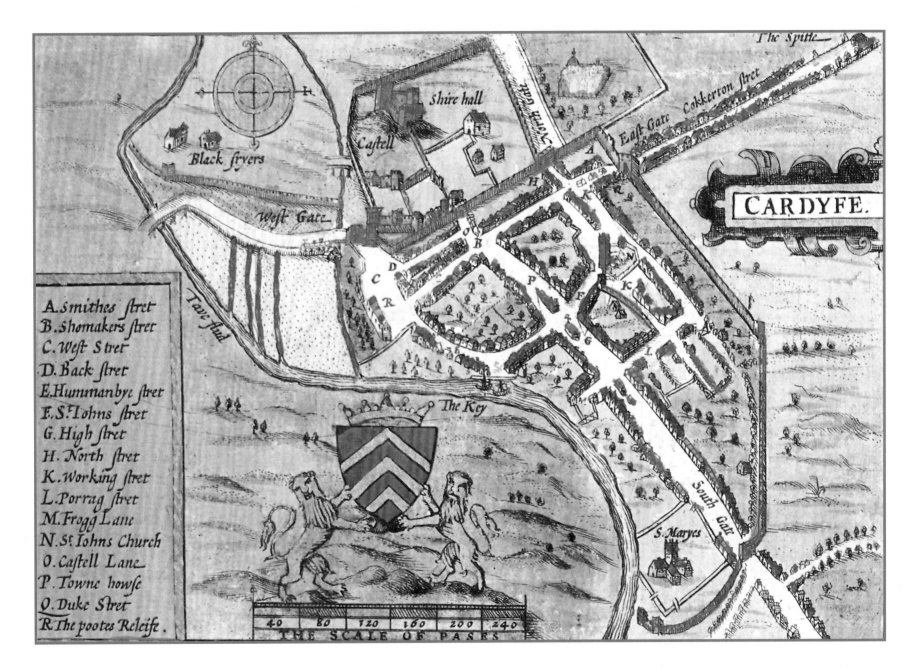

The Spitle

Cokkerton stret

Shire hall

Castell

East Gate

North Gate

CARDYFE.

Black fryers

West Gate

Tave flud

The Key

S. Maryes

South Gate

A. Smithes stret
B. Shomakers stret
C. West Stret
D. Back stret
E. Hummanbye stret
F. S. Iohns stret
G. High stret
H. North stret
K. Working stret
L. Porrag stret
M. Frogg Lane
N. St Iohns Church
O. Castell Lane
P. Towne howse
Q. Duke Stret
R. The pootes Releife.

| 40 | 80 | 120 | 160 | 200 | 240 |

THE SCALE OF PASES

133

CARDIGAN

'Scarce had the Normans setled their Kingdom in Britain but that they assailed this County, as well to enjoy so fair a possession, as to secure those Seas from any invasion against them: so that Rufus first wrested from the Welsh-men the maritime Coasts and Henry the first gave the whole County to Gilbert de Clare.

This Gilbert fortified Cardigan, the Shire-Town, with a Wall and strong Castle; whose aged lineaments do to this day shew the industry both of Nature and Art: for the Town is seated upon a steep bank, her South-side guarded with the deep River Tyuy, and passable no way but by a Bridge under the Castle. The walls take the advantage of the rising Rocks, and circulate the Town even round about. The Castle is higher built upon a Rock, both spacious and fair, had not storms impaired her beauty and time left her carkase a very anatomy. The walls range as thou seest, and are indifferent for repair having three ways for entrance, and contain in compass six hundred and fourscore paces: whose position for Latitude is set in the degree 52,33 minutes from the North-pole, and for Longitude from the first West-point by Mercator, in the degree 15, and 10 minutes.

The Air is open and somewhat piercing; the Soil is hilly, and (Wales-like) uneven: yet more plain and champion towards the Sea, then in the East or North of the Land. For besides that great and high hill called Plinillimon, a continual range of lesser doth shoot along, yielding in their Valleys both goodly rich pastures, and very large Pools, which being assisted with Springs from the Rocks, do branch themselves, as veins in tbe body, and make fruitful their passages unto the Sea. In Tyuy one of these, as Giraldus hath written, the Beaver hath been found, a creature living both by land and water, whose stones the Physicians hold in great price. His fore-feet are like unto a dog, but the hinder whole skinned, as is the goose: the dog-like serve him on shore for to run, and the goose-like as Oars give him swift motion in swimming: his tail, broad and gristly, he useth as a stern, wherewith on the suddain he can divert his swift floating course. But this creature in these parts a long time hath not been seen, whose room we may well say the Salmon hath possest, who still coveting into fresh water Rivers, at their down-right falls, useth this policy: He bendeth himself backward, and taketh his tail in his mouth, and with all his strength unloosing his circle on the sudden (as a lath let go) mounteth up before the fall of the stream; whereupon such water-falls are called the Salmons Leap: and in these Rivers many such Salmons are caught.'

¶ The title panel of the county map states 'Cardigan Shyre described with the due forme of the Shire-town as it was surveyed by I.S. Anno 1610'. This is one of the few references on any of the maps to Speed having done his own work on the town plans, although it is explained in the introduction that all those with a scale included were by him. The letters I.S. indicate Iohn Speed, though his name is spelled John Speede in the publisher's imprint on the same map. The letters J and I seem to be interchanged almost at will, and Speed's names are subjected to considerable variation throughout the atlas.

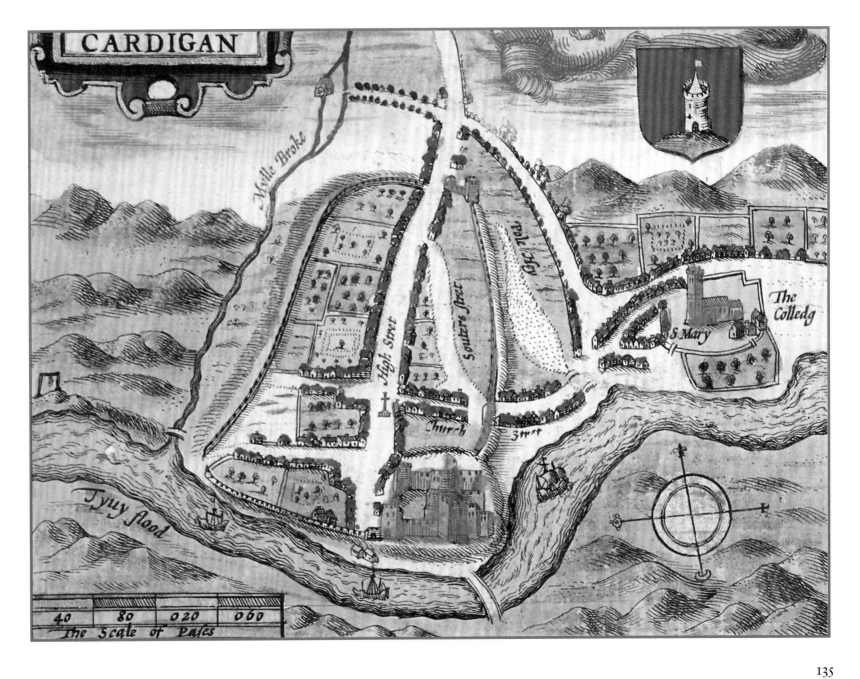

CARDIGAN

Mylle Broke

pole Hy

High Stret

Souters Stret

S. Mary

The Colledg

Church Stret

Tyuy flood

| 40 | 80 | 020 | 060 |

The Scale of Pases

135

CARMARTHEN

'The commodities of this Shire chiefly consist in Cattle, Pit-coal, Fowl and Sea-fish, whereof the Salmon is common among them, and that of such greatness and plenty as no place is better furnished therewith then the Shire-Town Caermarden.

Which Town by Ptolemy is called Maridunum; by Antonine the Emperour, Muridunum; by the Britains, Caerfridhin; and by us, Caermarden. It is pleasantly seated upon the South-West side of the River Touy, that runneth through the midst of this Shire, and falleth South from hence into the British Sea, where before times was a convenient Haven for Ships arrivage, but now is sore pestered with Sands and Shelfs: notwithstanding some small Vessels ascend up the River, even unto the Bridge of this Town, which is fairly built of free-stone. And over the same, upon a hanging rock, standeth a very large Castle, from whose stone-wall another intermingled with brick rangeth about the Town, being in circuit one thousand and four hundred paces. The Inhabitants of this place do not a little glory of their Merlin, who (as they say) was therin born, the son of a bad Angel, or of an Incubus spirit, the Britains great Apollo, whom Geffrey ap Arthur would rank with the South-saying Seer, or rather with the true Prophets themselves; being none other then a meer Seducer and phantastical Wizard: which howsoever Alani de Insulis in his Commentaries hath laboured to unlock those dark and hidden Similies, wherewith his Book is pestered and full, yet was it not without cause forbid the reading by the Council of Trent, as vain, and not worthy of countenance or credit.

At the entrance of the Normans this Town was brought under their obedience, and for a long time was distressed with the calamities of War, yet afterwards was made by the English Princes the Chancery and Exchequer for all South-Wales: and at this day is yearly governed by a Mayor, who ever after is an Alderman and Justice of the Peace, two Sheriffs elected out of sixteen Burgesses, all of them in skarlet, a Sword-bearer, a Town-Clerk, and two Serjeants with Maces: from whence the Pole is raised 52 degrees 15 minutes in Latitude, and for Longitude is in the degree 15 and 30 minutes from the first point in the West, according to Mercator.'

¶ The orientation of this plan shows north pointing to the normally south-west corner, no doubt so that the shape would fit neatly into the county map plate. This has possibly led to some confusion by Speed, for his text refers to the town being on the south-west side of the River Towy which is at variance with his plan. A number of uncorrected errors were inevitable in his atlas, bearing in mind the difficulties of travel and surveying, and the fact that most plates were engraved abroad.

CAERMARDEN

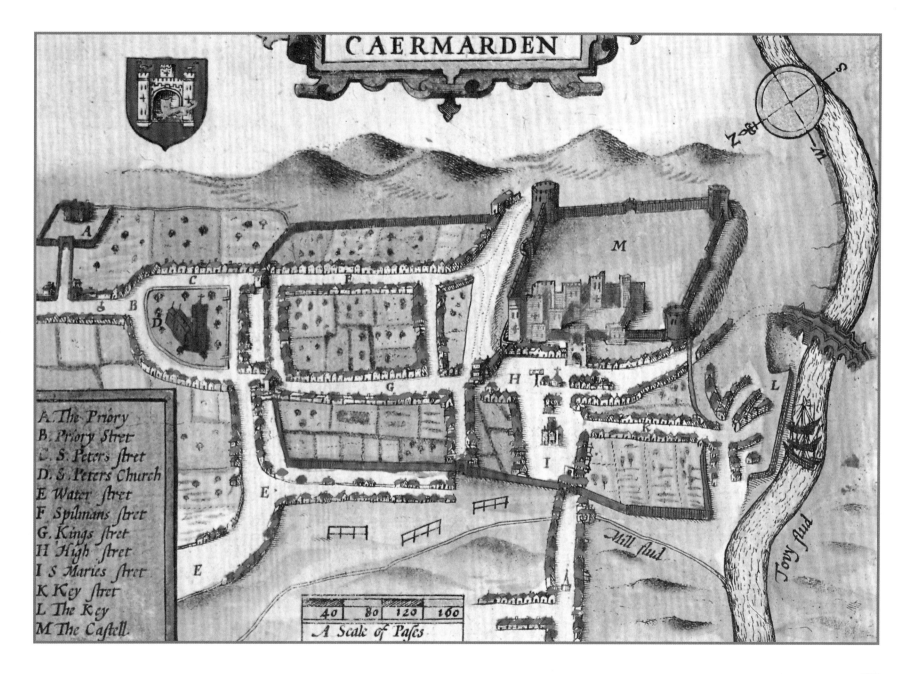

A. The Priory
B. Priory Stret
C. S. Peters stret
D. S. Peters Church
E Water stret
F Spilmans stret
G. Kings stret
H High stret
I S Maries stret
K Key stret
L The Key
M The Castell.

40 80 120 160
A Scale of Paces

Mill flud

Towy flud

DENBIGH

'Henry Lacy Earl of Lincoln, obtaining Denbigh by the grant of King Edward the first, after the conviction and beheading of David brother of Llewellin for high Treason, was the first that fortified it with a wall about, not large in circuit but very strong, and on the South-side with a fair Castle, strengthned with many high Towers. But he gave it over, and left the work unfinished, conceiving grief (as a sorrowful Father) that his only son came to untimely death, and was drowned in the Well thereof.

The fame of this Town spreads itself far for repute, as being reckonned the most beautiful place in all North-Wales: and it is of no less report, for the Castle adjunct unto it is impregnable for fortification. And this strange accident happening there in the year 1575 deserves not to be omitted, being left as a continual remembrance of Gods merciful providence and preservation at that time; That where by reason of great Earth-quakes, many people were put into great fear, and had much harm done unto them both within and without their houses, in the Cities of York, Worcester, Glocester, Bristow, Hereford, and in other Countries adjacent, yet in the Shire-Hall of Denbigh the bell was caused to toll twice, by the shaking of the earth, and no hurt or hinderance at all either done or received.

The government of this Town is mannaged by two Aldermen, and two Bailiffs, who are yearly elected out of twenty five Burgesses, that are their Assistants. It hath one Recorder, one Town-Clerk, and two Serjeants at Mace: and by observation of the Mathematicks, the Pole is elevated in the degree of latitude 53, and 49 scruples, and from the first West point in Longitude 16, and 45.'

❡ This is a slightly strange plan with the problems of combining overhead plan and birds-eye perspective giving an unbalanced result. The 'molehills' on the upper left contrast oddly with the northerly extensions of the plan. In the key, 'L' refers to 'the new church' which was then being constructed and appears in a part-built state; this remained its fate as it was never completed. It is still there today, more than 400 years later.

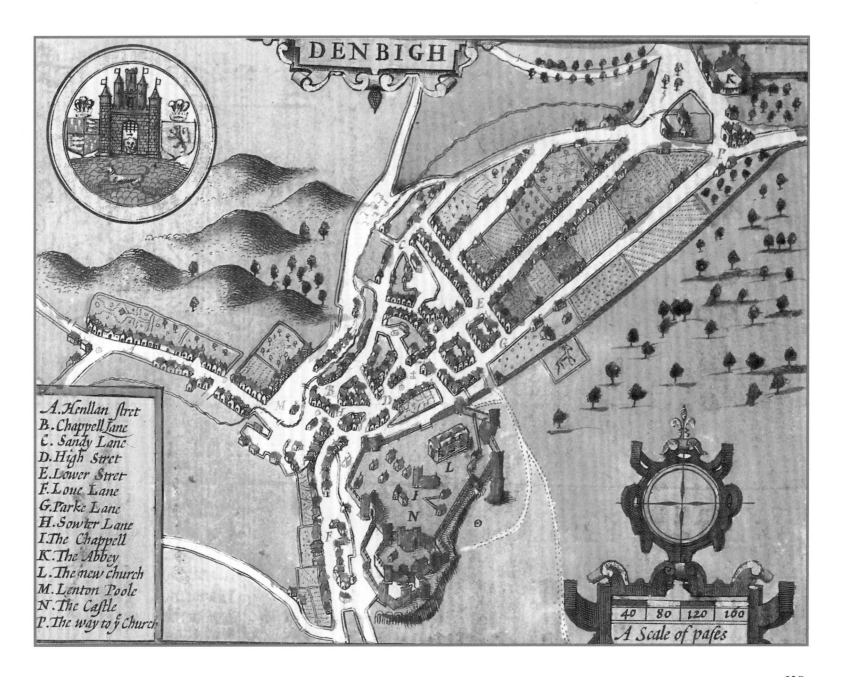

DENBIGH

A. Henllan ſtret
B. Chappell Lane
C. Sandy Lane
D. High Stret
E. Lower Stret
F. Loue Lane
G. Parke Lane
H. Sowter Lane
I. The Chappell
K. The Abbey
L. The new church
M. Lenton Poole
N. The Caſtle
P. The way to y̕ Church

40 80 120 160
A Scale of paſes

139

FLINT

'Places of defence are the Castles of Flint, Hawarden, vulgarly Harden, Treer, Rudland, Mold, Yowley, and Hope: of which, Flint and Harden are the two principal. The Castle of Flint, famous for the benefit it received from two Kings, and for the refuge and relief it gave unto the third. It was founded by Henry the second, finished by Edward the first, and long after gave harbour and entertainment to that noble, but unfortunate Prince, Richard the second, coming out of Ireland, being within her walls a free and absolute King, but no sooner without but taken prisoner by Henry Bullingbrook, Duke of Lancaster, losing at that time his liberty, and not long after his life. This standeth in the graduation of Latitude 53, 55 minutes, in Longitude 17.

This Country [County] hath many shallow Rivers in it, but none of fame and note, but Dee and Cluyde. Howbeit, there is a Spring not far from Rudland Castle, of great report and antiquity, which is termed Fons Sacer, in English, Holy-Well, and is also commonly called S.Winifrids Well, of whom antiquity thus reporteth, That Winifrid, a Christian Virgin, very fair and virtuous, was doated upon by a young lustful Prince or Lord of the Country, who not being able to rule his head-strong affections, having many times in vain attempted and tried her chastity, both by rich gifts and large promises, could not by any means obtain his desires; he therefore (in a place of advantage) suddenly surprized and ravished her weak (yet resisting) body. After the deed done, the cruel Tyrant, to stop her cries and exclamations, slew her, and cut off her head: out of which place did suddenly arise a Spring that continueth to this day, carrying from the Fountain such a forcible stream and current as the like is not found in Christendom.

Over the head of the Spring there is built a Chappel of Free-stone, with Pillars curiously wrought and ingraved; in the Chancel whereof, and Glass-window the Picture of the Virgin is drawn, together with the memorial of her life and death. To this Fountain Pilgrims are accustomed to repair in their zealous, but blind devotion; and divers others resort to bathe in, holding firmly that the water is of much vertue.

There be many red stones in the bottom of this Well, and much green moss growing upon the sides; the superstition of the people holding that those red spots in the stones were drops of the Ladys blood which all the water in the Spring can never wash away; and that the moss about the wall was her hair, which though some of it be given to every stranger that comes, yet it never wasteth. But howsoever this be carried for truth by the tradition of time, the moss itself smell exceeding sweet'.

¶ Apart from the unusual shape of the town, the main feature of Flint, both on the ground and in history, is the castle. It is perhaps best known as the place where Richard the Second's reign ended, and appropriately was featured by Shakespeare in his eponymous play. The view of St Winifred's Well appears on the map of Flintshire, and it is described in Speed's text.

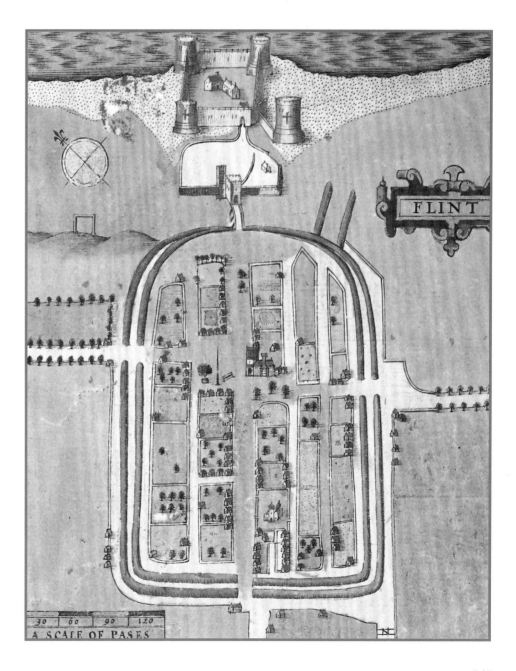

HARLECH

'Upon the West and Sea-shore of this Shire, Harlech a Market and Mayor Town standeth, bleak enough and barren, but only for Fowl and fish; houses not many, neither curiously built, wherein standeth a little Chappel decayed and without use, in which lieth buried Sir Richard Thimbleby, an English Knight, who for the delight he took in that game, removed his abode from a far better soil. Here also standeth a most strong and beautiful Castle, mounted upon a Hill, and with a double Bulwark walled about, commanding the Sea, and passage of entrance of such as seek to invade the Coast. And surely a great pity it is to see so fair a work fall to decay: the Constable whereof by Patent is ever the Mayor of this Town: near unto which are two great inlets of Seas, which at low water may be passed upon the Sands with Guides. Upon whose shore, as upon all the Sea-coasts in this County, abundance of Herrings are caught, for which cause they are much frequented in the season of the year by many people from divers Countries.

This Town being the chiefest of the Shire, the Pole shall be elevated only from thence, whose height for Latitude standeth in the degree 53.29. minutes and for Longitude in the 15.47.minutes.

In form this Shire [Merioneth] somewhat resembleth a Welsh-Harp, though small is the Musick that to her Inhabitants she makes, being the roughest, and most unpleasant to see to (as Giraldus their own Historian writeth) in all Wales. The Air for great pleasure, nor soil for great profit, I cannot greatly commend, unless it be for the many and mighty great winds, that for the most part therein do rage, and the spired hills clustered together so near and so high, as the same Author affirmeth, that Shepherds upon their tops falling at odds in the morning, and challenging the field for fight, before they can come together to try out the quarrel, the day will be spent, and the heat of their fury shut up with their sleep.' ❧

¶ The only plan to incorporate a mermaid, though the Beaumaris plan has a similar embellishment. Speed or his engraver included a number of fanciful figures and scenes in some of the maps, particularly those of the coastal counties, but very few in the plans. Harlech has little but the castle to commend it and sounds from the description to have been an inhospitable place. Note the uncorrected error in 'A s[c]ale of pases'.

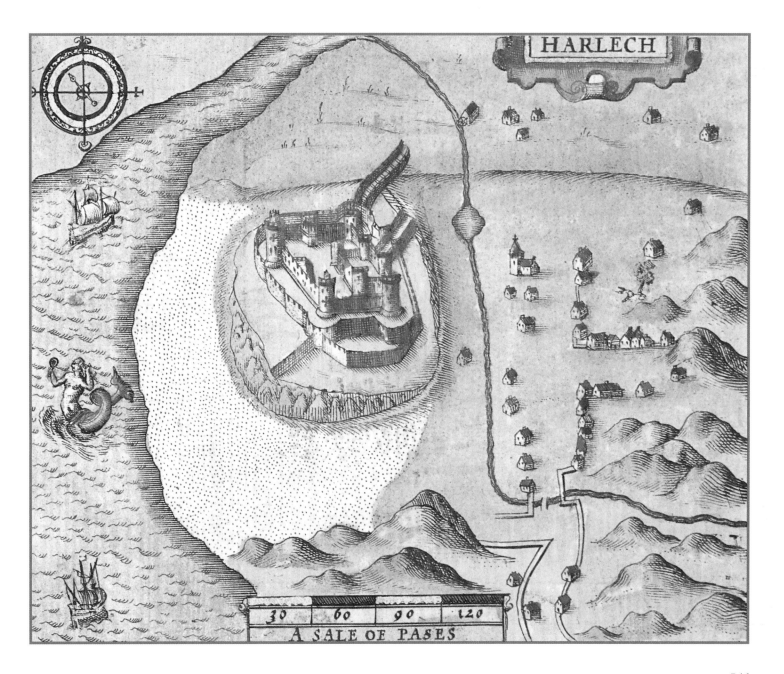

HARLECH

30   60   90   120

A SALE OF PASES

143

LLANDAFF

'In the same graduation [as Cardiff] almost is sited the City Landaff, wherein is a Castle and Cathedral, Church, dedicated to S. Telean, Bishop of the same, without any other memorable matter worthy the speaking of.

The air [of Glamorgan] is temperate, and gives more content to the mind, then the soil doth fruit or ease unto Travellers. The hills being high and very many, which from the North notwithstanding are lestened as it were by degrees; and towards the Sea-coast the Country becometh somewhat plain; which part is the best both for plenty of Grain, and populous of Inhabitants. The rest all mountain, is replenished with Cattel, which is the best means unto wealth that this Shire doth afford; upon whose hills you may behold whole herds of them feeding; and from whose Rocks, most clear springing waters through the Vallies trickling, which sportingly do pass with a most pleasant sound, and did not a little revive my wearied spirits amongst those vast mountains, imployed in their search: whose infancy at first admitted an easie step over; but grown unto strength, more boldly forbad me such passage, and with a more stern countenance held on their journey unto the British Seas: and Tave among these is accounted for a chief.'

¶ This is the only Welsh plan which does not show a scale of paces. This is surprising as Llandaff is so close to Cardiff that Speed should have found it a simple matter to survey it. It may be that he had access to an existing work and did not need to augment it. However, the description that follows indicates that the motive may have been the poor regard in which Llandaff was held by Speed and his contemporary historians. He certainly does not provide more than a passing reference to the place and maybe he passed it by deliberately, or having overlooked it, decided to give it dismissive treatment. The additional text referring to the county is included to offset the brevity of the Llandaff entry.

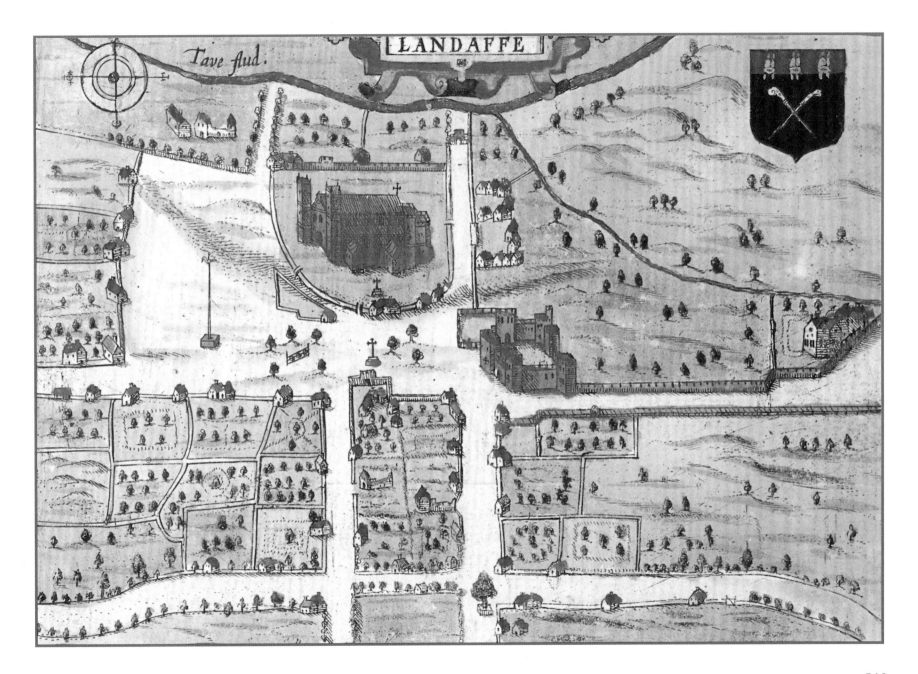

LANDAFFE

Tave flud.

145

Monmouth

'This City for beauty, circuit, and magnifical respect, is laid in the ruines of her own decay; neither may any more lament the loss of glory then Monmouths Castle, which captive-like doth yield to conquering time. Her down-cast stones from those lofty turrets, do show what beauty once it bare, standing mounted round in compass and within her walls another mount, whereon a tower of great heighth and strength is built, which was the birthplace of our Conquering Henry, the great triumpher over France, but now decayed, and from a Princely Castle is become no better then a regardless Cottage.

In this Town a beautiful Church built with three Iles is remaining, and at the East end a most curiously built (but now decayed) Church stands, called the Monks Church: In the Monastery whereof, our great Antiquary Geffrey, surnamed Munmouth, and Ap Arthur, wrote his History of Great Britain; whose pains as they were both learned and great, so have they bred great pains among the learned both to defend and to disprove.

The Towns situation is pleasant and good, seated betwixt the Rivers Monnow and Wye: three Gates yet stand, besides that Tower or Lock of the Bridge, and a Trench or tract of Wall running betwixt them on each side down to the River, containing in circuit about eight hundred paces.

The Town is in good repair, and well frequented, governed by a Mayor, two Bailiffs, fifteen Common-Counsellors, a Town-Clerk, and two Sergeants for their attendance. It is in latitude removed from the Equator 52 degrees and 8 minutes, and from the West point of longitude is set in the degree 17.36 minutes.'

¶ Being right on the English border and the county town of what had been created as an English county only 70 years before, it is understandable that on his splendid general map of Wales Speed shows Monmouth in Herefordshire. However, on the county map of Monmouth, the boundary is shown as being the River Wye at that point thus placing the town back in its own county. The two rivers shown on the plan are the Monnow and the Wye, with variations of the Latin 'fluvius' shown as 'flud' and 'flood', not necessarily indicating inundation.

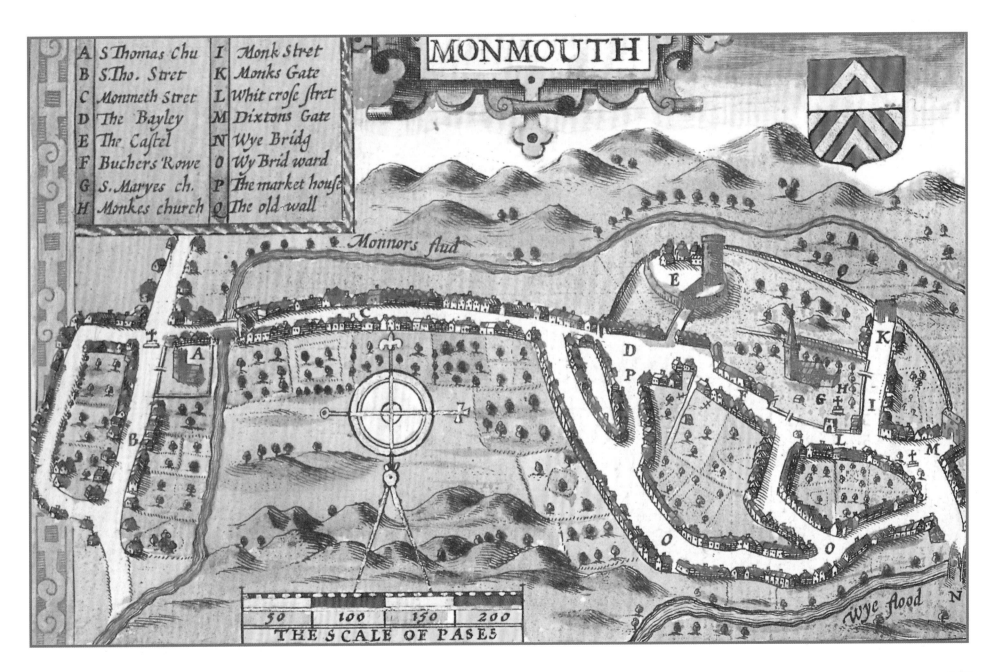

MONMOUTH

A	S Thomas Chu	I	Monk Stret
B	S Tho. Stret	K	Monks Gate
C	Monmeth Stret	L	Whit crose stret
D	The Bayley	M	Dixtons Gate
E	The Castel	N	Wye Bridg
F	Buchers Rowe	O	Wy Brid ward
G	S. Maryes ch.	P	The market house
H	Monkes church	Q	The old wall

Monnors flud

THE SCALE OF PASES

50   100   150   200

Wye flood

147

Montgomery

'Towns for Trades and Commerce in this County are six: the chiefest thereof and Shire-Town is Mount-gomery, very wholesom for air, and pleasant for situation, upon an easie ascent of an hill, and upon another far higher mounted, stands a fair and well repaired Castle, from the East Rock whereof, the Town hath been walled, as by some part yet standing, and the tract and trench of the rest even unto the North-side of the said Castle, may evidently be seen: whose graduation for Latitude is placed in the degree 53. and for Longitude 17. the lines cutting each other in the site of this Town.

This Town hath lately received the honour and title of an Earldom, whereof Philip Herbert the second son of Henry Earl of Pembroke was created the first, in Anno 1605.

The ancient Inhabitants that were seated in Guineth and Powisland, whereof this Shire was a part, were to the Romans known by the name of Ordovices, a puissant and couragious Nation, whose hearts and hills held them the longest free from the yoke of subjection, either of the Romans or English: for unto the days of Domitian, they kept play with the Romans, and were not brought to the will of the English before the reign of King Edward the first. Those Ordovices inhabited the Counties of Mountgomery, Merioneth, Caernarvan, Denbigh, and Flint, which are of us called now North-Wales, a people generous and of affable conditions, goodly for feature, fair of complexion, couragious of mind, courteous to strangers, and that which is most commendable, most true and loyal to the English Crown.'

¶ The map of Montgomeryshire has an imprint which states 'Described by Christopher Saxton Augmented and published by Iohn Speed …'. This is one of the occasions where Speed acknowledges the origin of the survey on which he based his map, although there is no consistency about this. He certainly was the originator of the town plan of Montgomery, as with all but one of the Welsh plans. Despite the modest size of the town there is a key provided, but not any orientation.

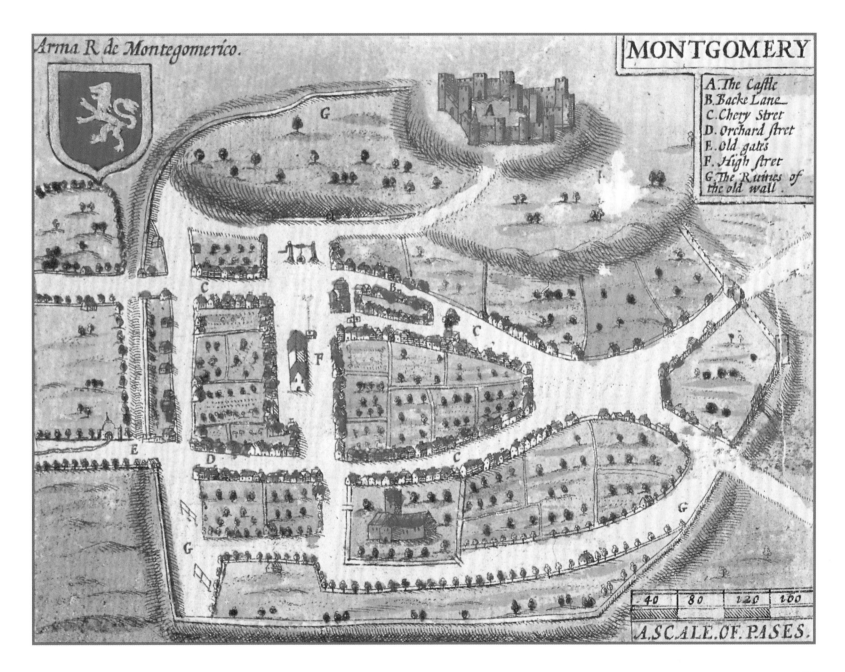

Arma R de Montegomerico.

MONTGOMERY

A. The Caſtle
B. Backe Lane
C. Chery Stret
D. Orchard ſtret
E. Old gats
F. High ſtret
G. The Ruines of
the old wall

40   80   120   160

A. SCALE. OF. PASES.

149

PEMBROKE

'The commodities of this Shire are Corn, Cattle, Sea-fish, and Fowl, and in Giraldus his days saleable Wines. The Havens being so commodious for Ships arrivage: such is that at Tenby, and Milford, an Haven of such capacity, that sixteen Creeks, five Bays, and thirteen Roads, known all by several names, are therein contained where Henry of Richmond, of most happy memory, arrived with signal hopes of Englands freedom from under the government of an usurping Tyrant.

Near unto this is Pembroke, the Shire-town seated, more ancient in shew then it is in years, and more houses without Inhabitants, then I saw in any one City throughout my Survey. It is walled long wise, and them but indifferent for repair, containing in circuit eight hundred and fourscore paces, having three gates of passage, and at the West end a large Castle, and locked Causey, that leads over the water to the decayed Priory of Monton. The site of this Town is in the degree of Longitude, as Mercator does measure, 14.and 55 minutes, and the elevation from the North-pole in the degree of Latitude 52.

The air is passing temperate, by the report of Giraldus, who confirmeth his reason from the site of Ireland, against which it butteth, and so near adjoined, that King Rufus thought it possible to make a bridge of his Ships over the Sea, whereby he might pass to Ireland on foot.'

¶ The absence of a key on this plan and that of St Davids is slightly surprising as Speed makes particular mention in the title cartouche of the Pembrokeshire map of his authorship, thus '...and the situations of Penbroke and St. Davids shewed in due form as they were taken by John Speed'. However both towns were so modest in size that there was not a great deal to be identified.

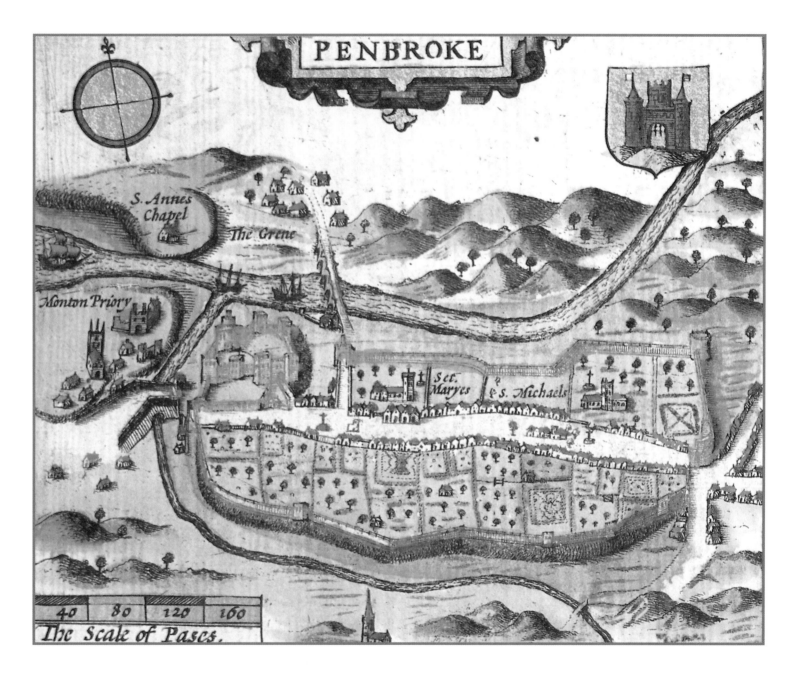

PENBROKE

S. Annes Chapel

The Grene

Monton Priory

Sct. Maryes

S. Michaels

| 40 | 80 | 120 | 160 |

The Scale of Paces.

151

RADNOR

'Places most worthy of note in this Shire are as insueth: The first is Radnor, from whom the County received her name, anciently Magi where the Commander of the Pacensian Regiment lay, and thought to be the Magnos in Antonine the Emperors Survey. This Town is pleasantly seated under a hill, whereon standeth mounted a large and strong Castle, from whose Bulwark a Trench is drawn along the West of the Town, whereon a wall of stone was once raised, as by the remains in many places appeareth. This trench doth likewise inverge her West side so far as the River, but after is no more seen: whose graduation is observed to have the Pole elevated for Latitude 52 degrees, and 45 minutes; and for Longitude, from the first point of the West, set by Mercator, 17 degrees and 1 minute.

Prestain for beauteous building is the best in this Shire, a Town of Commerce, wonderfully frequented, and that very lately. Next is Knighton, a Market Town likewise, under which is seen the Clawdh-Offa, or Offaes Ditch, whose tract for a space I followed along the edge of the Mountain, which was a bound set to separate the Welsh from the English, by the Mercian King Offa: and by Egbert the Monarch a Law made, by the instigation of his Wife, that it should be present death for the Welsh to pass over the same, as John Bever the Monk of Westminster reporteth: and the like under Harald, as John of Salisbury writeth; wherein it was ordained, that what Welshmen soever should be found with any Weapon on this side of that limit, which was Offaes Ditch, should have his right hand cut off by the Kings Officers. The fourth place for account is Raihader Gowy, who besides the great fall of Wye with a continual noise, hath her Markets there kept upon the Sabbath, which I there observed, and here note for an offence.'

¶ A simple plan, dominated by the castle, and lacking any key or names of buildings or streets. It also lacks any compass indication, though the plan appears to have been tilted slightly to the right. The reference at the end of Speed's description, to a Sunday market in Rhyader looks like an early example of whistle-blowing!

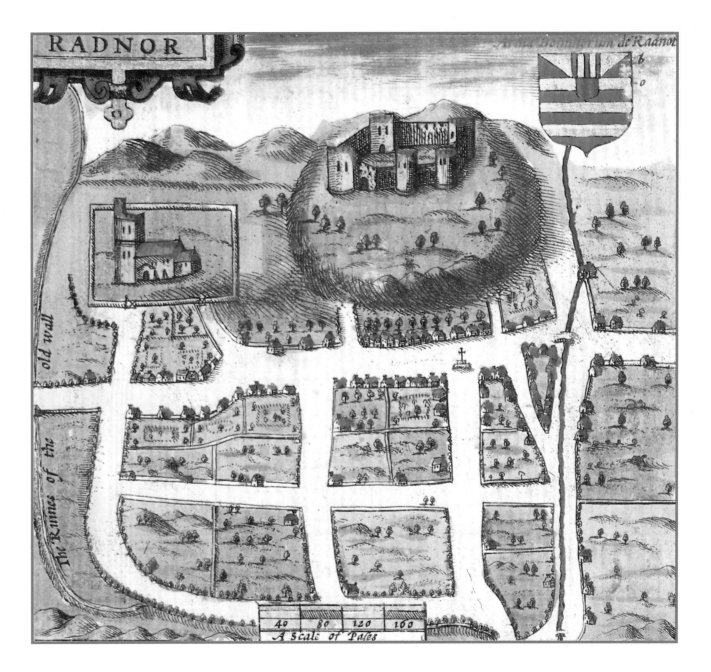

RADNOR

Arma Dominorum de Radnor

The Runnes of the old wall

40   80   120   160

A Scale of Paces

153

ST ASAPH

'Another like Monastery, but of lesser account [than Bangor] stood in the Vale beneath Varis (a little City placed by the Romans in the confines of this Shire and Denbigh-shire) and upon the Bank of Elwy and Cluyd: This the Britains call Llan Elwy, of the River; the Englishmen, Asaph, of the Founder, and the Historiographers, Asaphensis. It is more famoused for antiquity, then for building or bravery: for about the year 560 Kentigern Bishop of Glasco, being fled hither out of Scotland, placed here a Bishops See, and directed a Monastery, gathering together 663 in a religious brotherhood, whereof 300 that were unlearned gave themselves to husbandry, and to work within the Monastery; the rest of Prayer and Meditations. When he returned into Scotland he ordained Asaph, a godly and upright man, to be governor over this Monastery, of whom it took the name, and is called Saint Asaphs.

This Country is nothing mountainous, as other parts of Wales are, but rising gently all along the River of Dee, makes a fair shew and prospect of her self to every eye that beholds her, as well upon the River, being in most places thereabouts four or five miles broad, as upon the other side thereof, being a part of Cheshire. The Air is healthful and temperate without any foggy clouds or fenny vapors, saving that sometime there ariseth from the Sea and the River Dee, certain thick and smokey-seeming mists, which nevertheless are not found hurtful to the Inhabitants, who in this part live long and healthfully. The Clime is somewhat colder there than in Cheshire, by reason of the Sea and the River that engirts the better part of her; by which the Northern winds being long carried upon the waters, blow the more cold; and that side of the Country upward, that lieth shoaring unto the top, having neither shelter nor defence, receiveth them in their full power, and is naturally a Bulwark from their violence unto her bordering neighbours, that maketh the snow to lie much longer there than on the other side of the River. The soil bringeth forth plenty both of Corn and Grass, as also great store of Cattle, but they be little: To supply which defect, they have more by much in their numbers then in other places where they be bigger. '

¶ Both the plans on the Flintshire map are rather lacking in detail and information. This plan, like that of Flint, has nothing identified except the scale and orientation. The scale may be reasonably accurate, a 'pace' of Speed's measurement being 5 feet – or two normal strides, but the orientation would seem to indicate disorientation as the cathedral and town are east of the River Elwy and not as shown here.

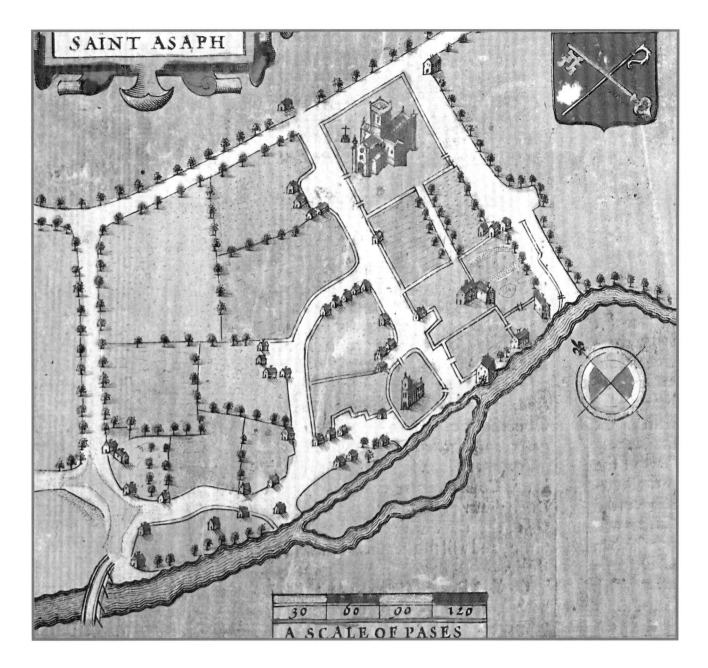

SAINT ASAPH

A SCALE OF PASES

30 | 60 | 90 | 120

155

ST DAVIDS

'A City as barren [as Pembroke] is old S.Davids, neither clad with Woods, nor garnished with Rivers, nor beautified with fields, nor adorned with Meadows, but lieth always open both to wind and storms. Yet it hath been a Nursery to holy men; for herein lived Calphurnius a Britain Priest, whose wife was Concha, sister to S.Martin, and both of them the Parents of S.Patrick the Apostle of Ireland. Deui a most religious Bishop, made this an Archiepiscopal See, removed from Isca Legionum, This the Britains call Tuy Dewy, the house of Deui; the Saxons, Dauyo Mynden; we S.Davids: A City with few Inhabitants, and no more houses then are inserted in the draught; yet hath it a fair Cathedral Church, dedicated to S.Andrew and David: in the midst of whose Quire lieth intombed Edmund Earl of Richmond, father to K.Henry the seventh: whose Monument (as the Prebends told me) spared their Church from other defacements, when all went down under the hammers of King Henry VIII. About this is a fair wall, and the Bishops Palace all of free stone, a goodly house I assure you, and of great receipt; whose uncovered tops cause the curious works in the walls daily to weep, and them to fear their downfal e're long.

But Monton the Priory, and S.Dogmels, places of devout piety erected in this County, found not the like favour, when the commission of their dissolutions came down against them, and the axes of destruction cut down the props of their walls.

This Shire hath been strengthned with sixteen Castles, besides two Block-houses, commanding the mouth of Milford Haven, and is still traded in eight Market-Towns.'

¶ As with many Welsh towns 400 years ago, St Davids had very few inhabitants. It was important only for its ecclesiastical establishment, and this is clear from Speed's plan. In his text he emphasises that he has shown every one of the few dwellings.

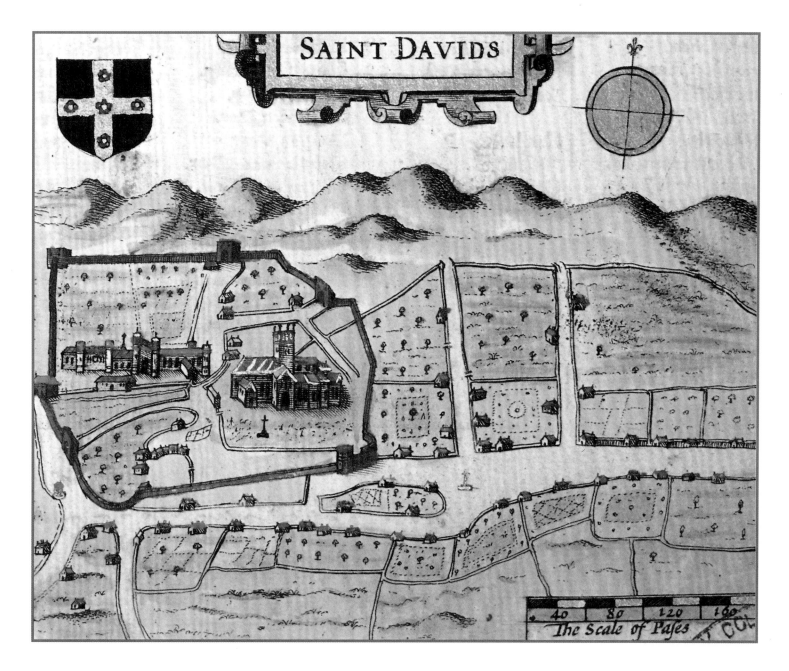

SAINT DAVIDS

40   80   120   160

The Scale of Paſes

157

The Scottish Town Plan

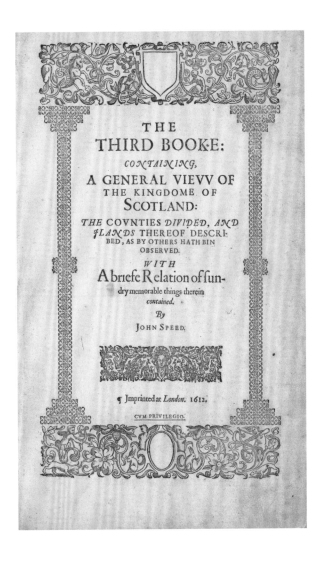

THE
THIRD BOOKE:
CONTAINING,
A GENERAL VIEVV OF
THE KINGDOME OF
SCOTLAND:
THE COVNTIES DIVIDED, AND
ILANDS THEREOF DESCRI-
BED, AS BY OTHERS HATH BIN
OBSERVED.

WITH
A briefe Relation of sun-
dry memorable things therein
contained.

By
JOHN SPEED.

¶ Imprinted at London. 1612.

CVM PRIVILEGIO.

EDINBURGH

'Scotland is fair and spacious, and from the South-borders spreadeth it self wide into the East and West till again it contracts it self narrower unto the Northern promontories: furnished with all things befitting a famous Kingdom; both for Air and Soil, Rivers, Woods, Mountains, fish, Fowl, and Cattle, and Corn so plenteous, that it supplieth therewith other Countries in their want. The people thereof are of good feature, strong of body, and of couragious mind, and in Wars so venturous, that scarce any service of note hath been performed, but that they were the first and last in the field. Their Nobility and Gentry are very studious of learning, and all civil knowledge; for which end they not only frequent the three Universities of their own Kingdom (S.Andrews, Glascow, and Edenburgh, the Nurseries of Piety, and mansions of the sacred Muses) but also much addict themselves to travel in foreign countries.

The Counties contained in this Kingdom are many, and every where bestrewed with Cities, Towns, and Burroughs, as is that of England: and, as England, I intended to describe it, had I not been happily prevented by a learned Gentleman of that Nation, [Timothy Pont] who hath most exactly begun, and gone through the greatest difficulties thereof, to build upon whose foundations I hold it injurious: and am so far from any ambition to prevent his noble purposes, that I heartily wish all happy furtherances thereto, with a longing desire to see, by his industrious labours, another Scene added to the perfecting of the Theatre of Britains Glory.

Yet, in the mean while, lest I should seem too defective in my intendments, let me without offence (in this third, though short Book) give only a general view of that Kingdom, upon observations from others; which to accomplish by mine own survey (if others should hap to fail, and my crazy aged body will give leave) is my chief desire; knowing the Island furnished with many worthy remembrances appertaining both unto them and to us, whom God now hath set under one Crown.'

¶ In his *Theatre of the Empire of Great Britaine* John Speed had not intended to include any material relating to Scotland when he first planned the work some 15 or more years before publication. Before the union of the Crowns in 1603 Scotland was not only alien territory but also unpredictable for travel. After the accession of James 1st it was no surprise that Speed, who was a zealous royalist, would not only dedicate the whole work to his sovereign but also include a fine map of 'The Kingdome of Scotland', albeit one copied from Mercator's map of 1595. The inclusion by Speed of vignettes of James I, Queen Anne and their two sons might appear rather obsequious, but certainly transformed an otherwise rather dull map into a splendid and highly prized cartographic item.

The representation of Edinburgh does not appear on the Scottish map, but on Speed's dramatic map of 'The Kingdome of Great Britaine and Ireland', balancing a view of London. John Speed made much use of the libraries of learned friends, and particularly that of Sir Robert Cotton. It was from this antiquarian's collection that Speed took the Edinburgh view, although its origins were before Queen Elizabeth came to the throne.

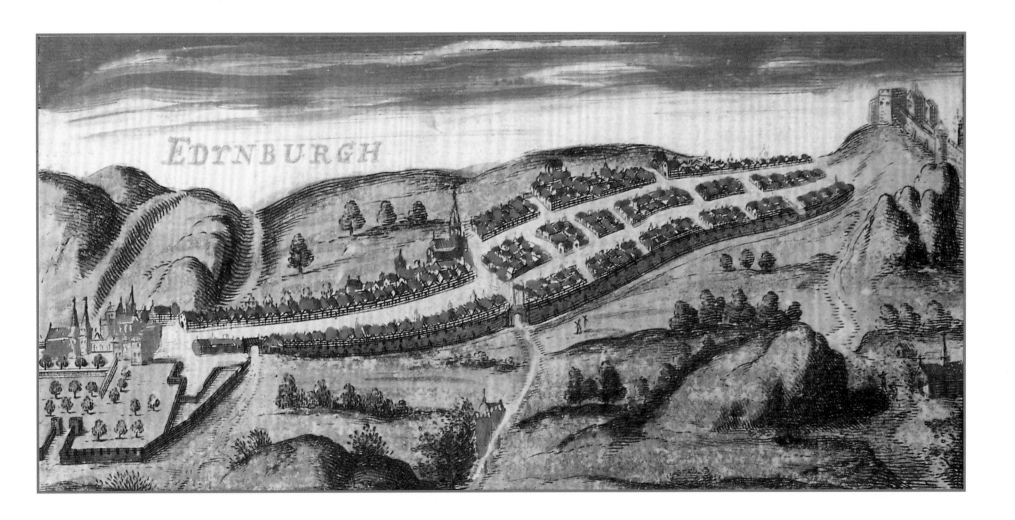

EDINBURGH

161

THE
FOVRTH
BOOKE:
Containing,
THE KINGDOME OF
IRELAND.

WITH
AN EXACT CHOROGRAPHICAL DIMENSION
OF THE PROVINCES THEREIN CON-
TAINED, AND THOSE AGAINE DIVI-
DED INTO THEIR SEVERAL
COVNTIES.

TOGETHER,
With a compendious defcription
of that *NATION*, and *ILANDS*
Commodities,
By
JOHN SPEED.

¶ Jmprinted at London by *William Hall*, 1612.
Cum Priuilegio,

CORK

"Near unto the River that Ptolemy called Daucona, and Giraldus Cambrensis (by the alteration of some few letters) nameth Sauranus and Sava enus, which issueth out of Muskery Mountains, is seated the City of Cork, graced also with another Episcopal Dignity (and with the Bishops See of Clon annexed unto it) which Giraldus calleth Corragia, the Englishmen Cork, and the native Inhabitants of the Country Coreach.

This town is so beset on every side with neighbouring molesters, as that they are still constrained to keep watch and ward, as if there lay continual siege against it. The Citizens of this place are all linkt together in some one or other degree of affinity, for that they dare not match their daughters in marriage into the Country, but make contracts of matrimony one with another among themselves.

In this place that holy and religious man Briock is said to have his birth and breeding, who flourished among the Gauls in that fruitful age of Christianity, and from whom the Diocess of Sanbrioch in Britain Armarica, commonly called S.Brieu, had the denomination.

Although since the time of S.Patrick, Christianity was never extinct in this Country, yet the government being haled into contrary factions, the Nobility lawless, and the multitude wilful, it hath come to pass, that Religion hath waxed (with the temporal common sort) more cold and feeble, being most of them very irreligious, and addicted wholly to superstitious observations: for in some parts of this Province, some are of opinion, that certain men are yearly turned into Wolves, and made Wolf-men. Though this hath been constantly affirmed by such as think their censures worthy to pass for currant and credible; yet let us suppose that happily they be possessed with the disease and malady that the Physicians call Lycan-thropi, which begetteth and engendereth such like phantasies through the malicious Melancholy: and so oftentimes men imagine themselves to be turned and transformed into forms which they are not.'

¶ The blank shield on this plan remained so throughout the many editions of the atlas despite many other additions, amendments and alterations being made to a large number of the plates. It may be that Speed intended, as with the majority of the English and Welsh town plans, to include the coat of arms of each place, but did not fulfil this intention. None of the Irish plans include heraldry, so Cork's blank space may have been left in place through oversight.

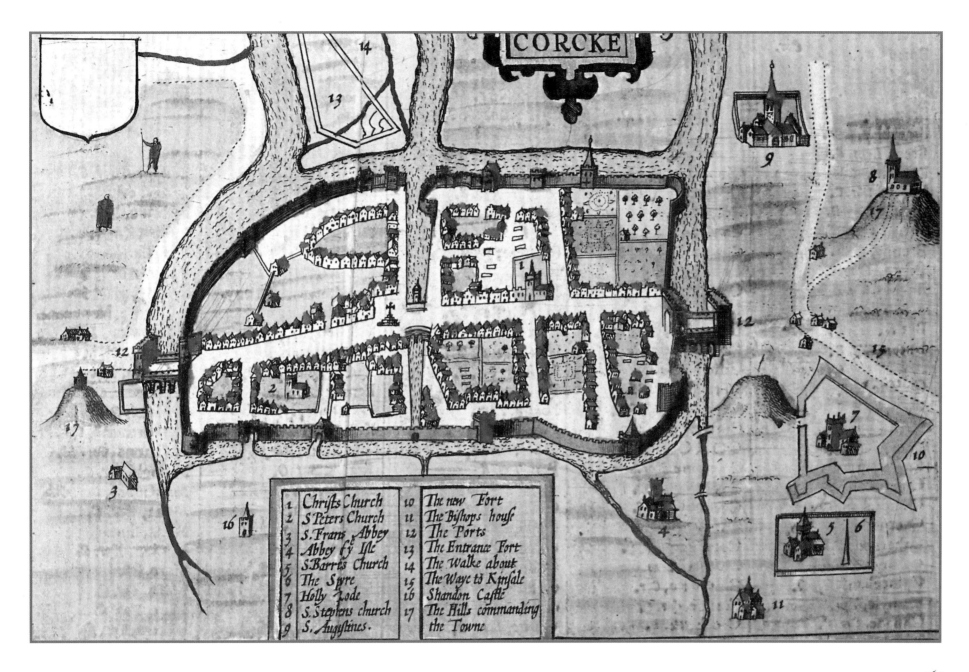

CORCKE

1	Chrifts Church	10	The new Fort
2	S Peters Church	11	The Bifhops houfe
3	S. Frans Abbey	12	The Ports
4	Abbey fy Ifle	13	The Entrance Fort
5	S. Barres Church	14	The Walke about
6	The Spyre	15	The Waye tó Kinfale
7	Holly Rode	16	Shandon Caftle
8	S. Stephens church	17	The Hills commanding
9	S. Augustines.		the Towne

DUBLIN

'The City which fame may justly celebrate alone, beyond all the Cities or Towns in Ireland, is that which we call Divelin, Ptolemy, Eblana; the Latinists Dublinium, and Dublinia; the West-Britains Dinas Dulin; the English-Saxons in times past, Duplin; and the Irish, Balacleigh, that is, the Town upon hurdles: for it is reported that the place being fennish and moorish, when it first began to be builded, the foundation was laid upon hurdles.

This is the royal seat of Ireland, strong in her munition, beautiful in her buildings, and (for the quantity) matchable to many other Cities, frequent for traffick and intercourse of Merchants. In the East Suburbs, Henry the second, King of England caused a royal Palace to be erected: and Henry Loundres, Archbishop of Divelin, built a store-house about the year of Christ 1220. Not far from it is the beautiful colledge consecrated unto the name of Holy Trinity, which Queen Elizabeth of famous memory dignified with the priviledges of an University. The Church of S.Patrick being much enlarged by King John was by John Comin Archbishop of Dublin, born at Evesham in England, first ordained to be a Church of Prebends in the year 1191. It doth at this day maintain a Dean, a Chanter, a Chancellor, a Treasurer, two Arch-Deacons, and twenty two Prebendaries.

This City in times past, for the due administration of civil government, had a Provost for the chief Magistrate. But in the year of man's Redemption 1409 King Henry the fourth granted them liberty to chuse every year a Mayor and two Bailiffs, and that the Mayor should have a gilt Sword carried before him for ever. And King Edward the sixth (to heap more honour upon this place) changed the two Bailiffs afterwards into Sheriffs: so that there is not any thing here wanting that may serve to make the estate of a city most flourishing.

As the people of this County do about the neighbouring parts of Divelin come nearest unto the civil condition and orderly subjection of the English; so in places farther off they are more tumultuous, being at deadly feuds amongst themselves, committing oftentimes man-slaughters one upon the other, and working their own mischiefs by mutual wrongs.'

¶ The capital city of Ireland would have been reasonably accessible to Speed and this is the only Irish town plan that is based on his own survey. The copious references in the key, and the inclusion of a compass bearing show the attention that was given to this plan, and Speed was clearly impressed by Dublin and probably spent longer there than in many other places.

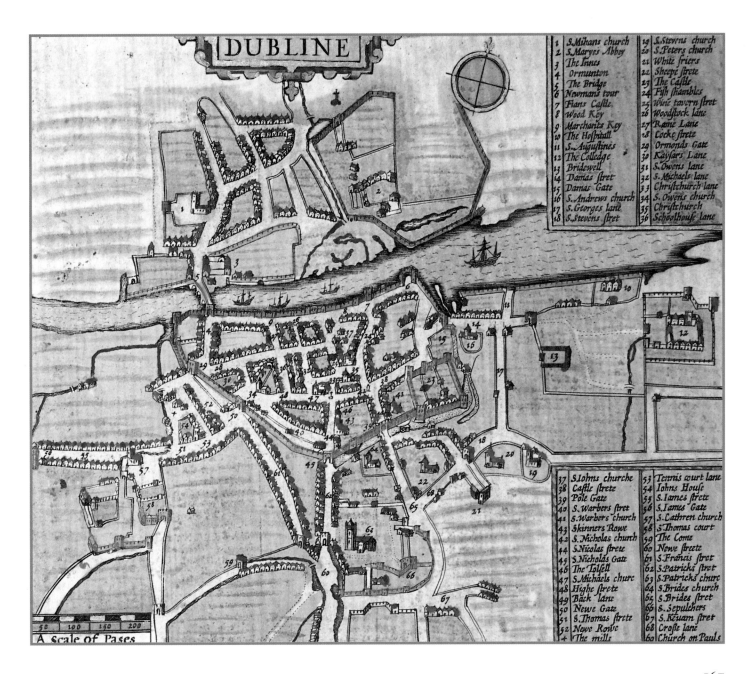

GALWAY

'The principal City of this Province [Connaught] and which may worthily be accounted the third in Ireland, is Galway, in Irish, Gallive, built in manner much like to a Tower. It is dignified with a Bishops See, and is much frequented with Merchants, by reason whereof, and the benefit of the Road and Haven, it is gainful to the Inhabitants to traffick and exchange of rich Commodities, both by Sea and Land. Not far from which, near the West shoar that lies indented with small inlets and out-lets, in a row are the Islands called Arran, of which many a foolish fable goes, as if they were the Islands of the living, wherein none died at any time, or were subject to mortality; which is as superstitious an observation as that used in some other corners of the Country where the people leave the right arms of their Infants males unchristned (as they term it) to the end that at any time afterwards, they may give a more deadly and ungracious blow when they strike: which things do not only show how palpably they are carried away by traditious obscurities, but do also intimate how full their hearts be of inveterate revenge.

This County as it is divided into several portions, so is every portion severally commended for the soil, according to the seasonable times of the year. Twomond or the County Clare, is said to be a country so conveniently situated, that either from the Sea or soil there can be nothing wisht for more, then what it doth naturally afford of it self, were but the industry of the inhabitants answerable to the rest. Galway is a Land very thankful to the painful husbandman, and no less commodious and profitable to the Shepherd.

The Air is not altogether so pure and clear, as in the other Provinces of Ireland, by reason of certain moist places (covered over with grass) which of their softness are usually termed Boghes, both dangerous, and full of vapourous and foggy mists.'

¶ This is one of the few plans to provide no information at all except pictorially. The remoteness of Galway made it inevitable that Speed would use an earlier plan if one existed, and despite its anonymity this plan adds considerably to the map of the Province of Connaught.

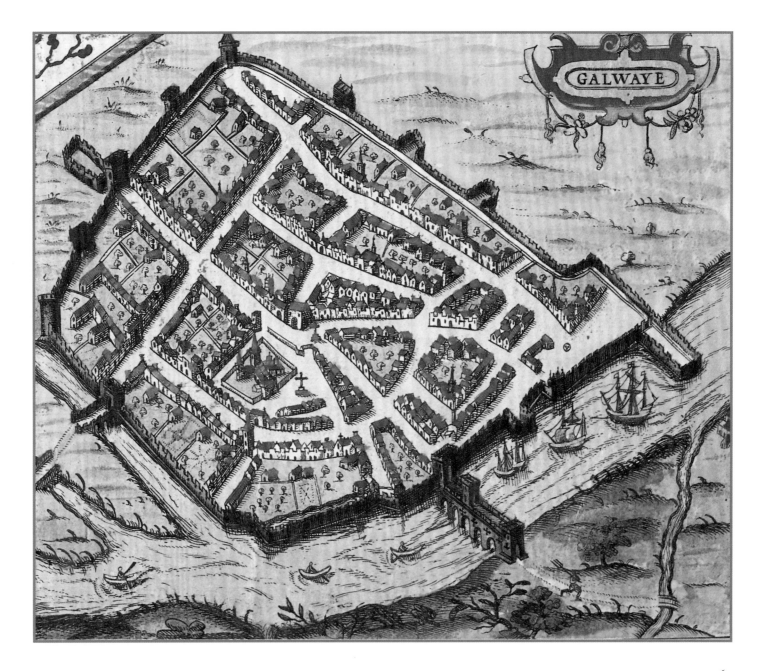

GALWAYE

169

LIMERICK

'The principal City of the Province [Munster] is Limerick, which the Irish call Loumeagh, compassed about with the famous River Shennon, by the parting of the Channel. This is a Bishops See, and the very Mart-town of Mounster. It was first won by Reymond le Gross an Englishman, afterwards burnt by Dunewald an Irish Petty King of Thuetmond. Then in process of time Philip Breos an Englishman was infeoffed in it, and King John fortified it with a Castle, which he caused therein to be built. In this Castle certain Hostages making their abode in the year 1332, grew (as is reported) so full of pride and insolency, that they slew the Constable thereof, and siezed the Castle into their own hands. But the resolute Citizens that could neither brook nor bear with such barbarous cruelty, did in revenge then shew such manly courage and vivacity, as they soon after recovered the Castle again, repaying the Hostages in such hostile manner, as that they put them all to the Sword without partiality.

The position of this Town is by Mercator placed for Latitude 53 degrees 20 minutes; and for Longitude, 9 degrees 34 minutes.

The general commodities of this Province are Corn, Cattle, Wood, Wool, and fish. The last whereof it affords in every place plenty and abundance of all sorts. But none so well known for the store of Herrings that are taken there, as is the Promontory called Eraugh, that lies between Bantre and Ballarimore Bay, whereunto every year a great fleet of Spaniards and Portugals resort (even in the midst of winter) to fish also for Cods.'

¶ The map of the Province of Munster is the only one of the four Irish provincial maps to include two town plans, the other being Cork. The plan of Limerick has a key identifying 14 landmarks, (Cork 17) but they both lack orientation. The Key letters M and N were transposed.

KEY

A St Iohns Streete and gate
B The thye Bridge
C The Maine Streete of the Citty
D New gate
E Our Ladies Church
F The key
G The Kinges castle
H Thomond bridge
I St Frances Abbey
K St Peters
L St Dominicks Abbey
N The Bishops house
M St Monchius church
O St Michaells church

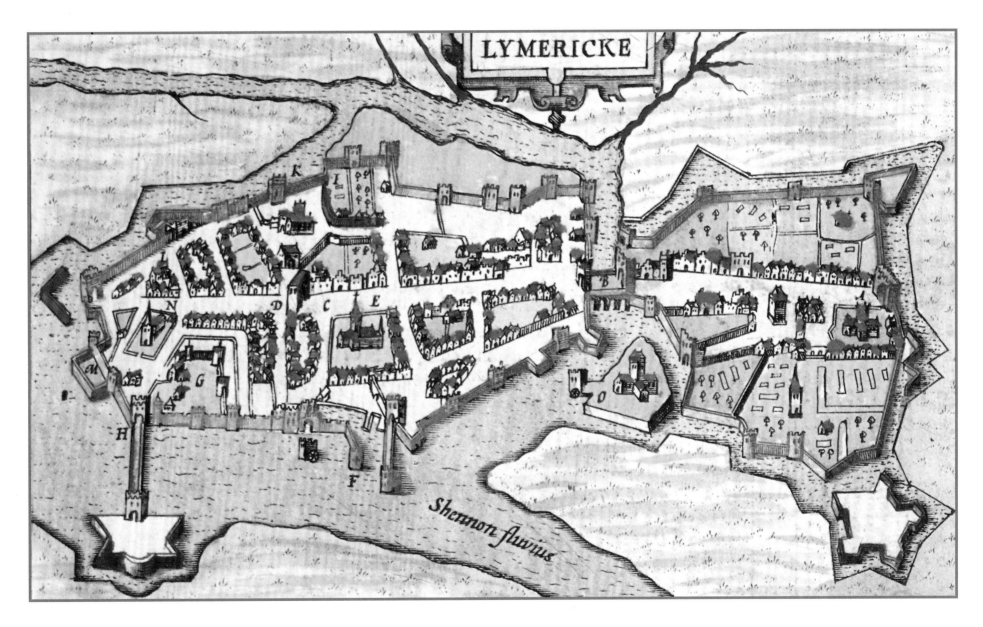

LYMERICKE

Shannon fluuius

SELECT BIBLIOGRAPHY

R.A. Skelton, 'Tudor town plans in John Speed's Theatre', *The Archaeological Journal*, vol.108, 1951.

Illustrated Road Book of England and Wales. The Automobile Association, 1961

R.A. Skelton, *The County Atlases of the British Isles, 1579-1703*. Carta Press, 1970.

R.V. Tooley, *Maps and Map Makers*. Batsford, 1970.

John Hadfield, *The Shell Guide to England*. Michael Joseph, 1970.

P.J. Radford, 'What makes Speed so special...', *Art and Antiques*, pp.22-6, 19 May 1973.

T. Chubb, *Printed Maps in the Atlases of Great Britain and Ireland*. Dawson, 1977.

R.V. Tooley, 'John Speed: a personal view'. *The Map Collector*, 1, 1977.

Nigel Nicholson, *The Counties of Britain: a Tudor atlas by John Speed*. Pavilion, 1988.